The Hallet Family of Cape Cod

By Charles Clark
2007-08

Brandon Weissler: Editor, Transcriber

William P. Quinn: Photojournalist, Contributing author

II

Dedications

- **This is book is dedicated to my grandfather, Matthews C. Hallet, and my mother, Mary G. Clark.**
-
- **Other dedications**
-
- Cassie and Candy Bule for helping with the museum.
-
- William Quinn for all of his help with this book and the glass-plate photographs.
-
- Noel W. Beyle for recognizing Matthews C. Hallet's collection.

Preface

This book is a view of old Cape Cod by true Cape Codders. Unlike other Cape Codders, the Hallets have the history that has been captured in a time where people live for the moment. They have opened the door for all to see how their ancestors looked and lived. The glass-plate photograph collection inside puts you into the 1800s and while hearing the stories about that period, we all can appreciate what was it like. While we enter Cape Cod to take upon the five villages in Yarmouth and connect to our past, these photographs portray our very own ancestors living out their legacies. Through the findings in this book, we can witness true family bonds and through their homes and letters, we can only try to interpret their feelings at that time. The Hallet Family of Cape Cod has opened a window to just a small part of their archives of Cape Cod history. The glass-plates and other artifacts the Hallet family possesses are of great value, but it is the meaning and the sharing of history where the true worth lies.

Copyright Page

ISBN: **978-1-4276-2118-4**

Telephone: 508-362-3362
Website: www.hallets.com

Published by the Hallet Museum
139 Old Kings Highway
Yarmouthport MA, 02675

Contents

Thacher Taylor Hallet, better known as T.T., helped pioneer the development of Yarmouthport in the late 1800s. He wore many hats during his time, as T.T. was an entrepreneur, world traveler, a Justice of the Peace, Selectman, Postmaster, Tax Collector, collector of customs, and a pharmacist. It was that pharmaceutical profession that led to him building Hallet's store in 1889 in Yarmouthport on Cape Cod, Massachusetts. Hallet was born May 14, 1853 and died in 1930.

Matthews C. Hallet, named after his grandfather, was born May 26th, 1905 where he grew up in Yarmouthport and was a graduate of John Simpkins High School. Matthews would eventually marry his childhood sweetheart, Mary, who was born in 1908. The couple endured the hardships of the Great Depression and World War II. They also worked side by side throughout their marriage of nearly 50 years. Mary died in January 1977, and Matthews would join her 5 months later, dying of a broken heart.

T.T.'s granddaughter, Mary Grace Hallet Clark ran Hallet's store from 1977 until 1998 when she passed away. Beloved in the town of Yarmouth, she kept the store just the way she inherited it from her parents. She was an associate member of the Rod & Gun club, the Friday Club of Yarmouthport, and the Congregational Church of Yarmouth and Yarmouthport and had worked for Cape and Vineyard Electric in their office. Mary was just a simple and proud woman who helped create the Hallet Museum so anyone could enjoy the old time treasures that she loved so much.

The Hallet Family of Cape Cod

The life, the times, the stories, the tradition.

Hallet's Store was built in 1889 by Thacher Taylor Hallet, was also known as the town pharmacist, Justice of the Peace, Selectman, Postmaster, Tax Collector, and the collector of customs. What is now primarily a sandwich and ice cream shop, T.T. then filled prescriptions and sold sundries on the side at Hallet's. Upon his death in 1930, his son Matthews Crowell Hallet took over the business with his mother. Then in 1938, along side his wife, Mary, they decided to turn to a then newly installed soda fountain, along with sundaes and sandwiches as their primary source of income. Many of the sandwiches were sold to local fisherman who would pass through Yarmouthport on their way to Chatham. Matthews C. would be in at 7 am when the coffee and donut crowd arrived, and with only midday breaks, ran it until 10 at night. As time changed, the toothpastes, razor blades, and paten medicines were taken over by pharmacy chains. Magazines and newspapers sales faded away as well since they could not compete with other venues, so food and ice cream became the Hallet moniker. His grandchildren helped periodically in the summer seasons. One of them became very interested in how Hallet's operated, and later on would take over the business. Matthews C.'s mechanical ability was limited to a screwdriver and a hammer, so when things stopped working, they were no longer used. So since his grandson was a mechanic by trade, he would be amazed that all of his old equipment could be repaired. When Matthews C. and his wife passed away in 1977, their only daughter Mary Hallet known as Mary G Clark ran the store and her son, Charles (the grandson previously mentioned), became involved in it again in 1989 as the store became 100 years old. The Hallet Museum was created shortly after to show the glass plate photograph collection that is a big part of the museum. The museum also provided a home for old documents, which once was also the old town meeting place and the one time office of the former Massachusetts Senator, the Honorable John Simpkins. Mary and Charles had preserved everything from the original oak drawers, cabinets, and trays that once held T.T.'s medicines and compounds.

Where time and environment continually changed around it, Hallet's store remains virtually the same. Yarmouthport was completely different 100 years ago. Family units remained whole as divorce was uncommon and six-day workweeks were the norm. The center of the community was governed more by the people than by politics. Every family played a role in how communities were developed.

The Hallet's role dominated Yarmouthport from sea captains to printing to building homes along 6A. The Hallet family even had a role on the board of the golf club in Cummaquid, the creation of the port off of Wharf Lane and Yarmouth's first freezer plant. Let's not forget the storage facility on Railroad Avenue, as Yarmouthport was the hub and central part of distribution of goods and hardware.

Old Yarmouth's beginnings also involved the Hallet family. Andrew Hallet came to Yarmouth in 1637 where he was one of the first founders of Yarmouth and owned about two hundred acres of land. His farm was located in Yarmouth, but now is considered to be the northwestern part of Yarmouth and the northeastern part of Barnstable. He had five children; Andrew Jr., Samuel, Hannah, Josias, and Joseph. Andrew Hallet Jr., was also a large landowner just like his father. He owned about three hundred acres of some of the best land going from the Barnstable line to a quarter mile east of that on both sides of Hallet Street, which got it's name from his family.

THE KODAK.

ANYBODY can use the KODAK. The operation of making a picture consists simply of pressing a button. One Hundred instantaneous pictures are made without re-loading. No dark room or chemicals are necessary. A division of labor is offered, whereby all the work of finishing the pictures is done at the factory, where the camera can be sent to be re-loaded. The operator need not learn anything about photography. He can *"press the button"* —*we do the rest.*

Send for copy of KODAK Primer, with sample photograph.

THE EASTMAN DRY PLATE AND FILM CO.,
Price, $25.00.   ROCHESTER, N. Y.

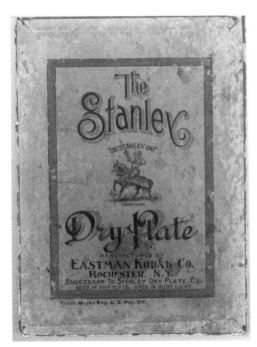

The collection of Matthews C. Hallet was created to remember one great man in Yarmouthport for his effort of preserving a glass-plate collection of his ancestors. Nathan T. Hallet originally gave these glass-plates to Matthews C. Hallet, and since the collection was very large and heavy, Matthews needed a wheelbarrow to bring them home. As the dusty old plates sat in the closet in Matthews home, renowned author and photojournalist William P. Quinn approached him and requested processing them in order to make them into photographs. As the photos were being identified, the collection of Matthews C. Hallet was created. There were only three copies made. One belonged to Matthews, one to William Quinn, and one was donated to the Yarmouth Historical Society, where they sat in a drawer for years. The glass-plates themselves were still maintained by Matthews C. There were 109 of the prints processed in 1975, and today there are now over 230 glass-plates that exist in the collection. After the passing of Matthews C., the glass-plate collection was given to Charles Clark, his grandson. Mary, Matthews' daughter, would proceed to identify the collection through the work of William P. Quinn and another author, Noel W. Beyle. As Mary continued to identify the prints, they were published in the *Yarmouth Register Newspaper*. Through Mary's effort to honor her father, a stamp was made to protect against reprints. For years, the photos have been on display in books, magazines, and newspapers, and the byline would always be to honor Matthews C. Hallet. As the true keeper of this great collection, Charles Clark, along with his mother Mary, created the Hallet Museum in 1990. The museum would provide a home and site for the collection of Matthews C. Hallet. These prints may be viewed and bought in the Hallet Museum and will have the official stamp of the Matthews C. Hallet collection to verify authenticity.

The box camera and tripod were the only means of taking pictures in the early 1800s and were the typical operation setup for glass plate photography. This sophisticated process required great detail of what you were capturing, and most images were prearranged to limit a photographer's mistake. With the detailed work of the photographer, one would need to be properly dressed right down to the appropriate flower on your lapel. The workings of the camera consisted of the tools of the bellows in her hand and the black cloak cloth to block out the light to see what she was photographing. As photographs capture images, they also capture time, where as you admire the camera in this photo, it also indicates the time of the season. This early spring adventure captured a brief moment of the early 1800s. These photographs are logged onto glass plates like program files on computers, and with that we have the option of interpreting the brief image of what time of year it was, and the time of day. These pioneers set forth the first wave of capturing time. The photographs that these cameras provided would forever change how we would view history.

The processes involving taking photographs incorporated this big sophisticated camera where it required a clean environment since any dust or debris would cloud the lens or the plate. Light was key to the quality of the shot and photographs at night were almost unheard of. When night shots were taken, they were dangerous since the flash was provided by gunpowder. As the camera was setup on the tripod, and the photographer shrouded the lens with the black cloak to view the image that was upside down, they meticulously took the time to insert the glass plate negative and when the conditions were right through the shutter, it exposed the image to the glass plate. The process was then to transport this back so it can then be developed. There were bath-type solutions to expose the image on the glass plate, which would then be transferred onto photographic paper.

Photo by H.K. Cummings and provided by William P. Quinn

(Through the eyes of the Matthews C. Hallet's glass plate & photo collection)

On December 7, 1941 mother and I had been for our Sunday afternoon ride, to see my grandfather. We came home and Dad greeted us with ill-fated news of Pearl Harbor. I was kind of stunned at the thought that Japs had declared war upon us. I pondered over it for a while and then shook it out of my mind. Of course in a small town where I live the people need something to hash over most of the time. The older people are genuine Cape Codders who have never been outside their own community for many years, can prophecy the world's future and what is to come by their renowned drugstore philosophy. Being around these people made me think more that the country was at war and the people in it. I didn't take much interest in

Mary at 137 Main Street in Yarmouthport with her dog Jon

what they said. Sometimes I got myself wrapped up in arguments on the war. I seemed to think I knew it all for I had heard someone else say so or perhaps I remembered it from the last news broadcast I had heard about three weeks ago. I never read a newspaper so I couldn't have read it. I never touch the things, furthest I get are the funnies and the pictures. We have been in the war now over a year. The men and women in this community started a listening post, now governed by the Army, it is part of the First Intercenter Command. Men, women and children are all airplane spotters. I go there by myself, it should bring the war nearer to me, but does it? Not especially, to me it seems a duty, just a part of daily living. Besides airplane spotting we have dim out every night. I am the official curtain puller. I don't think it has ever occurred to me that these curtains mean two things, if I <u>don't</u> pull them it might mean a convoy is apt to be sunk, subs creep in along the shores, and that Cape Cod is an inhabited place. By doing my job right it has the possibility of meaning that many lives would be saved, the enemy didn't get all the information they wanted and that my own life is safer. Do I realize why doing these few of many things, <u>why</u> they have to be done? Of course I don't and many of my friends are with me. I don't worry much. I ask for some new clothes or can I go to the movies or a dance tonight. Again do I realize that there is gas rationing, a pleasure-driving ban, and that the money for unnecessary clothing could go to buy war bonds? What do you think? Your answer will be right. I know I have been told over and over, "you haven't lost <u>anything</u> yet," or "you don't know the <u>half</u> of it." Me! Why I answer with a great big, "Yes sir," wanting very badly to spit in the person's face saying, "who cares?" But I will learn sooner or later that they were right. Now this little community in which I dwell is a regular stay-at-home little place. Knit for the soldiers and attend the weekly club meeting but by golly for a little bit of entertainment we can listen to the old radio which by now is tearing the hair out of our mother's head in hunks.

Mary G. Hallet in 1948

A monthly tour is out to the barn to visit old Bessie who sits on four blocks with an old dried up wreath dangling from the radiator cap with the vague inscription in the center, "Rest in Peace." While sitting by the radiator robed in four sweaters and two blankets wrapped firmly around you pitying the furnace who with a few exhausted grunts is trying to pump up a sizzling 65 degrees. All of a sudden a great commotion is heard outside. We look at each other thinking or rather hoping the war must be over. We make a dash for the front windows and disappointment fills the room as a C. card breezes by. Butter, sugar, and coffee have signed their lease to get out of our house, the date isn't set yet but no doubt it will practically sneak up on us (…might be next to be rationed off). To see a piece of steak would only be a mirage but I have eaten a little hamburg lately. Don't get alarmed it's only dignified horse meat. After eating if you feel as if a veterinarian would be welcome most any minute. Vegetables aren't too hard to find as last year we planted a Victory Garden. Don't you just love the "we," I had nothing to do with it. Well, another is planned for this year but the dreadful things how I hate to work in them. This year I am going to make myself work in it after all, maybe I'll like it, who knows? After I sit and think a while I certainly do live in a pretty good country even though it seems cruel sometimes and here after I hope I will realize that this country is at war and it is up to me to help fight even if not in the front lines.

So…until next time…Mary G Hallet (age 14)

A fuel-oil ration stamp issued in 1944

The following is transcribed letter written by Mary G. Clark in 1995 about her childhood memories

Main Street in Yarmouthport, the old Lyceum Hall building.
It is now a resident home.

Did you ever wonder what took place in Yarmouth and Yarmouthport in the war years of 1941 to 1945?

We are standing on the sidewalk watching a convoy from Camp Edwards slowly wind its way down Kings Highway. The convoy moved slowly down what is now 6A to arrive at the training grounds in the lower Cape.

As young girls it was fascinating to watch and wave to the soldiers. Sometimes they threw out spent shells with their addresses inside. Just a hint to get us to write letters.

Hallet's store was a busy place because of the soldiers (Yankee division) being stationed at Lyceum Hall. They were in charge of patrolling the beaches, and also watched for any suspicious looking people, especially with cameras.

Mary had four children: Gordon, Matt, Jon, and Charles. Aside from the demanding job of raising four children, she was also a secretary of the Cemetery Department.

Gas was rationed along with meat, fuel oil, butter and sugar. Ration stamps were issued out to all families so they could feed their families and keep them warm.

My father was a blackout warden, and every night curtains were up at the windows so no light shown through. Not even a cigarette butt was allowed.

We also had a Listening Post, which was manned by the residents of Yarmouth and Yarmouthport of all ages to detect foreign planes and report them. The post was down in back of the farm, two-hour shifts, twenty-four hours a day, after the war, all that served got a commendation. I still believe it was a good lesson for all of us in the younger generation. We learned to do without, and knew we had rules to obey. The enemy was very dangerous.

On V-J Day it was a big celebration and I rode with my dad in a big parade in a model A Ford, what fun the celebration was for young and old. The war was over.

Automobiles
By M. C. Hallet
John Simpkins High School
June 26, 1925

Matthews C. Hallet's car in back of Hallet's store

The history of the automobile is the United States is not very long. It has progressed with improvements very rapidly.

George B. Selden is an important factor in the commercial and industrial history of the motor vehicle in the United States. In 1895 he was granted an American patent for his invention of the clutch, and a combustion engine. His patent, or claim on his invention, gave him control over the automobile industry. Other men in the automobile business brought trial and Selden in 1911 lost his license and the control of his automobile patent.

An automobile board of trade was then organized to look into the general interest of the industry.

This industry grew very fast. Most of the factories were started in the Middle West. Detroit is now one of the greatest automobile cities of the United States and in the home of perhaps two-thirds of all American-made cars. There is a total of 164 automobiles manufactured in the United States. Some of the manufacturers make trucks; and the total number of makers is 188.

When automobiles were first brought into use, no one thought that they would be as practical as they are today. This incident, which happened about 1908, was told to me and it concerns three men in this town who drove from Boston in a Rambler Car. They left Boston for Yarmouth, and it took them a day and a half to get here. A flat tire in Brockton made it necessary for them to spend the night in that city, and they did not reach Yarmouth until the next morning. Today the same trip is made in about four hours.

The uses of a car, as everyone has seen, are very important. New York, which is the largest city in the world, has over a million pleasure cars; the state of Massachusetts has over half a million. Then there are the truck lines, which carry freight on short hauls cheaper and more conveniently than the railroads, and much faster than the old horse of yesterday.

Auto racing is one of the greatest sports of the United States, especially in the Middle West. Just recently, out of Indianapolis, the 500-mile race was held and was won by De Pavle in a Dussenberg. De Pavle traveled at the average speed of 101 miles per hour covering the distance of 500 miles in 4 hours, 56 minutes, 39 seconds, the fastest record for this distance. Last year the average speed was 98 miles per hour. The Dussenberg was equipped with balloon tires and they proved very successful.

Still another use of the automobile is for traveling. One of the first of the travel-bus lines in this country was started in the state of California. Finding this method successful, many bus-lines have been started in the East. A new bus-line was started this last winter running between Boston and New York. The price is about two dollars cheaper than by train.

People sometimes wonder what has made so many cars of such practical use today. If I should mention every detail it would be very interesting, so I will tell you only a few. First, everyone knows the convenience of a self-starter, a very clever invention. Among the very latest inventions are four-wheel brakes, which are on all the new cars; also balloon tires, which make riding a pleasure, are coming into use more and more every day. Soon every new car will be equipped with them.

The biggest improvement is in the style of the cars. Since the building of the first car the models have been changed every year. The aim has been to make the car look more sporty, which today is represented in the long, low models; or to make the car more comfortable. This resulted in the sedan, the coach, and coupe and the brougham

What is the cheapest car to run, that looks nice? Almost every one is asking this question, when gas is twenty-five cents a gallon.

You have all seen the Ford, and almost everybody has one. I won't say that it is not expensive to run, because all cars; but if you know how to take care of a car it will do the work for you. The best part of the Ford car is that you can buy parts for it at almost any place, at a comparatively low cost. That is why you see a Ford everywhere you go.

Now, take the Packard Straight-Eight for a car that looks as much as it costs. You surely must have an income to run one of these cars. Then there is the Rolls Royce car, which costs a considerable sum. However, the motor does not have to be touched for three years; it is only necessary to put in gas and oil. If the engine gives any trouble within the three-year limit, the company will give repairs.

Main Street going east in Yarmouthport. On the right is the Town Crier building.

Henry Ford, the automobile man of today, also has another car, which is more expensive, this is the Lincoln. All of you know that when you buy a car you always have to buy some additional equipment; as, for example, tires, bumpers, automatic windshield wiper, and other accessories. But when you buy a Lincoln car you have the most completely equipped car in America.

There are many other cars on the market, and there is a great deal of competition in the selling of them.

Considering the vast number of cars, which have been manufactured, and the improvements, which have made during the few years of the history of the automobile, it is only natural to expect many new improvements in the future. This present century expects new timesaving, laborsaving and money-saving devices, and the automobile has been one of the best illustrations.

Matthews C. Hallet

Graduation, J.S.H.S. – 1925
June 26, 1925

The Whale's Tooth, an antique shop run by Bob Lavery, which was leased to him by Matthews C. Hallet, and was located right next door to Hallet's store. Here we see (from left to right) Matthews C. Hallet, Bob Lavery, and Ronnie Baker. The two children, Rachael and Sarah, are Lavery's. They look ready for battle don't they?

Stories told by Bob Lavery

Yarmouthport Parade

On the 4th of July, 1974 another quiet beach day, Ron Baker, my daughters Rachel and Sarah, Matt and me, all had a great picture taken of us in front of the shop in assorted uniforms before Yarmouthport had it's first and only Fourth of July Parade in recent history. It was small, but enthusiastic with Patriotic parade flags and all. It went from my shop to Connolly's General Store* for Italian Subs and then back to my shop for a quiet lunch with all the participants. Hard to believe but we were applauded by all who viewed this small act of Patriotism as we "marched" along 6A to Connolly's.

*Connolly's General Store no longer exists. Today it is a doctor's office.

Another Cape Cod Summer Day

It was a hot July or August day, and Matthews and I were sitting on the wooden platform in front of my shop in two rocking chairs on a quiet, hot, beach day. The shop was small, so I used to load the platform with furniture so people could move around in the small area. Well, while we were sitting there a Lincoln Continental with 2 men and 2 women from New York pulled up to the empty curb with it's windows shut and the AC running and down comes the electronic window with a 60-ish balding man sitting in the passenger seat who called out to me, "Excuse me, are you a native here?" I looked at Matt and then back to him and said, "Does it look like I have a BONE IN MY NOSE???" The guy looked at the driver then back at me and said I guess I deserved that one! And off they went without directions...

What goes BANG in Yarmouthport
A Story about Bob Lavery by Charles Clark

Being around 15 years old at the store, I was hanging around and all of a sudden I heard this huge BANG. I went outside and Bob Lavery set up a miniature black powdered cannon between the two buildings and lit it off. I was amazed at the noise this thing made. He commences to reload another cannon, first goes in black powder, then a wad of toilet paper, which was then pushed down by a stick. Then he propped the cannon up on the driveway and then poured black powder into a little hole. With a cigarette tied to a stick that lit the black powder, a huge flash came out over the cannon and a second big bang occurred. The celebrations never stop in Yarmouthport.

In the early history of the town there was much that differed from present conditions. Reaping was done with the sickle. The clothing and the coverings for the beds were of wool or flax and chiefly made at home. The large and small spinning wheel, the hatchel, cards and the loom were a necessary part of the household furniture. The beds were filled with straw or feathers. The women made their own soap, and the tallow candles, which, with whale oil, supplied the light, were of domestic manufacture. There were no friction matches. The tinder, flint and steel sufficed to kindle the fire. There were no clocks at first. Hourglasses were used, as well as sundials. The houses built fronting the south so that the shadow of the chimney would indicate noon. There were no stoves. The houses had large chimneys with enormous fireplaces where the family in winter nights could sit on either side of the fire of green wood, which burned between huge fore and back logs. The crane and pothooks, the spit, the andirons and bellows were necessary apparatuses. If the

back of the dweller when facing the fire was cold, he could warm it by turning it to the blaze. A feature of each house was the brick oven built into chimney, heated by building a fire in it. In it, when the fire was drawn, the pies and cakes, the pudding and pots of beans, and the loaves of brown bread were placed on Saturdays, to be cooked by the slowly diminishing heat, which lasted through the night. The earlier inhabitants did not seek the main roads as sites for their houses. They preferably built near ponds where good water was at hand or on the shores of the bays convenient for fishing. Markets did not exist. Fresh meat was obtainable in the fall when a hog or a beef animal was killed for winter use. At other times a fowl, a calf or a sheep of the domestic stock might be used, or the "beef cart" patronized, which once or twice a week came to the door. While efforts were earlier made to check the excessive use of intoxicating liquors, the idea of total abstinence did not take root until about 1830 or later. Before that a supply of Medford rum was a necessary part of the winter's stock and on days of general training or other public occasions liquors were supplied on the spot or at the tavern. Sunday was strictly observed. Churchgoing was obligatory and could be enforced by law. The Puritan Sabbath resembled that of the Jewish faith from whom it was borrowed. It began at sunset Saturday night and ended at sunset Sunday night. A bride was expected to carry to her new home an outfit for housekeeping largely made with her own hands. The men wore knee breeches, and their hair was braided in queues. The tailoring was done by women. The boots and shoes were made by the cobbler of the neighborhood. The chairs were of domestic manufacture, bottomed with flags. The travel, when not on foot, was on horseback, the man in front on the saddle and the women behind on the pillion. Sometimes oxcarts were used. Carriages for pleasure or comfort were late in coming. At first they were two-wheeled chaises. I have been told by my elders that the first chaise in town (probably about 1800), and long the only one, was owned by Squire Sears.

In the early years there was little money. Taxes were collected in kind and transactions were carried on by exchange. Some English silver was in circulation and Spanish silver also appeared. The first bills of credit of the province, which appeared before 1700, became soon depreciated, and were known as the "old tenor." Other issues, known as "middle" and "new tenor," followed. In 1749 the value of the old tenor was fixed by law at a little over one-eighth of its face value in silver, and the middle and new tenor at about one-half. During the Revolution the Continental paper was also rapidly depreciated, until in 1780 it was worth only one-thirtieth of its face in silver, and it ultimately became worthless. Prices became very high, and they attempted to regulate them by law, as has so often been attempted before and since, and no doubt with a like result. The town voted August 16, 1779, to appoint a committee to fix prices and wages. This committee reports on the 6th of September. The meeting approved the schedule presented and voted that anyone violating it should be deemed an enemy of the country and treated as such.

There were few safe means of investment, and those who had money hoarded it. Luxuries were not entirely wanting. Some families had silver spoons and other articles brought from Boston or abroad, and gold beads for the ladies were not wholly absent. A writer in 1802 says: "The inhabitants are very industrious. The women are engaged in the domestic employments and manufactures usual in other parts of Massachusetts, and a number of them in curing fish at the flake yards." If we substitute "cranberry bogs" for "flake yards," this description will not be far astray today.

The conditions of the ancient life had their beneficial effects. Not only the spirit of self-help was called out, but mutual helpfulness was a necessity and must have softened the harder side of humanity which the stern struggle for a somewhat isolated existence would tend to foster. The care of the sick appealed to all, and while there were no trained nurses, the neighborhood produced men and women experienced in watching and caring for the sick according to the light of the times. House raisings, sheep sheerings and husking brought the people together in social meetings with amusement and jollity, as the church services did in a more serious mood. The poor were always present. At first when help at home did not suffice they were farmed out to those citizens who would take them for the least sum per week or year, having the benefit of their services. Later the town bought for an almshouse and poor farm the house and farm of James Taylor in West Chatham that had belonged to his father, Samuel Taylor. This house and its successor built by the town were managed by keepers and the town's poor cared for there until 1878, when the house and farm were sold and a new almshouse established next to the Baptist church.

Hallet Family Tree

Some of the books of the Hallet family tree indicate that the family dates back to as early as 1615, which predates when America's first settlers came in 1620. The origin of the Hallet name roots from England, and would then become the major influence that set Yarmouth and Barnstable. As our family tree shows, Howes, Bassett, Eldridge, Crowell, and Taylor were also of the larger Cape Cod families. The papers indicated here show the Hallet, Bassett, Eldridge, and Howes families were neatly recorded up until 1814. One family member spent a lot of time and effort in tracking their history. The Hallet entries would show the families that would marry, sometimes four or five times due to death. They would have large families with several children, however the records would show that some of the children died at an early age. These documents are prior to any government or town records.

15

Ships, Fishing, and Traveling

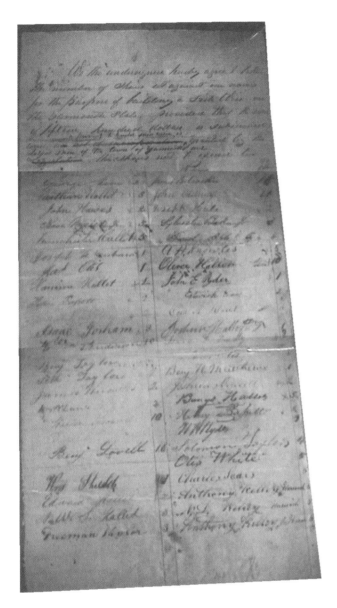

The Hallet family has a lot of great finds, and as we know Yarmouthport had a port. This is a photograph of an old fishing weir document from the late 1800s that can be found in the Hallet Museum. In this document, all of the old sea captains and members of the town signed and donated money to establish the weir. Names like: Captain Bangs Hallet, Seth Taylor - the tax collector, Nathan Hallet, and Oliver Hallet all had roles in the development of the weir.

As some have long forgotten, 6A and Old Kings Highway was once named Hallet Street. Yarmouthport was from the Cummaquid and Old Barnstable line, to where the fire station is today. Hallet street ran from the Barnstable and Cummaquid line up around the corner to where Summer Street, which was called Hawes Lane, and to around where Thatcher Street was. The port was in the area of this village.

The artist is unknown for this painting of the Wharf, but it appears to have been painted be mid to late 1880s. The landscape shows the church on the hill in Yarmouth and also looks towards Scargo Tower in Dennis. The documents (Weir and Walking Plank) are believed to pertain to this Wharf.

We the undersigned herby agree to take the number of shares in against our names for the purpose of building a Fish Weir on the Yarmouth Flats. Provided thus the sum of fifteen hundred dollars is subscribe, and a permit to build said weir is granted by the selectman of the town of Yarmouth and the shares not to exceed ten dollars each.

Names	No of Shares	Names	No of Shares
George S. Holmes	20	James B. Crocker	10
Nathan Hallet	5	John Eldridge	10
John Hawes	2	Joseph Hale	2
Isaac Myrick Jr.	5	Sylvester Baker Jr.	3
Manchester Hallet	5	David Gale? Jr.	6
Joseph H. Gorham	1	A. H. Knowles	5
Goe. Otis	1	Oliver Hallet	10
Harrison Hallet	2	John E. Ryder	1
John Bafsett	2	Estrovick Evans	2
Chris Bassett	2	Eben. A. Hallet	3
Isaac Gorham	3	Joshua Hallet Jr.	1
W.M. Anderson	10	Isaac F. Smalley	3
Benj. Taylor	3	(Undetermined) Otis	5
Seth Taylor	2	Benj. H. Matthews	1
James Knowles	2	Joshua Bassett	2
W.P. Davis	2	Bangs Hallet	5
Watson Crowell	10	Henry Bafsett	2
Joseph P. (Undetermined)		W.M. Ryder	3
Benj. Lovell	10	Solomon Taylor	4
		Otis White	5
W.M. (Undetermined)	1	Charles Sears	5
Edward Hallet	2	Anthony Kelley, Harwich	5
(Undetermined) T. Hallet	3	N.D. Kelley, Harwich	5
Freeman Taylor	3	Anthony Kelly Jr., Harwich	5

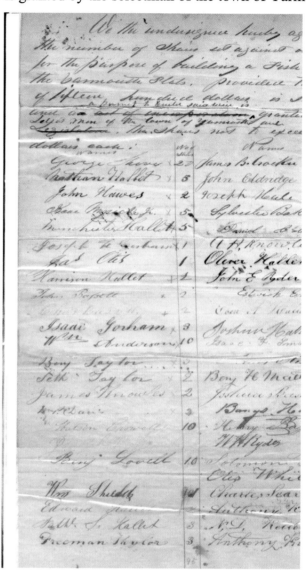

In the late 1800s, this document, which is printed on cloth, is believed to have created the pier of off Wharf Lane. For $1,500 in that time period, the pier would have been to be of very large size. This is only one of the documents that could have created the pier

Fish were very plentiful in the 1800s and could be harvested by the shoreline in the fish weir. Fish farming was practiced in the low shallow inlets where the fish used to come in and were trapped in the nets, where they were then harvested into the horse and buggy and delivered straight from the water right to your table. The tide would rise 8 to 10 feet and therefore the fish would be trapped.

We the undersigned agree to pay Thacher T Hallet as treasurer, on or before Sept. 10th 1892. The sum placed opposite our respective wears for the purpose of building a good plank walk or pier to a point at or near the outer end of the old long wharf. Said walk or pier to be finished on or before May 15th 1893 or the money to be returned

Geoff Simpkins	Pd. 25.00
Gorham Bacon	Pd. 25.00
H.G. Thacher	Pd. 25.00
R.E. Holmes	Pd. 25.00
R.W. Rigers	Pd. 25.00
Ruth Simpkins	Pd. 10.00
Mabel Simpkins	Pd. 10.00
T.T. Hallet	Pd. 10.00
Leo. Hallet	Pd. 5.00
Phillip Smith	Pd. 5.00
Hm. Shields	Pd. .50
Nathan Bassett	Pd. .50
Francis Alger	5.00
B.A.H.	1.00
Sophia Rogue Rufus Rogers	
Florence G Hoover and Mollie Kumees	Pd. 7.75
J.J. Simpkins	
Mabel Bacon	Pd. 1.00
(Undetermined) Bacon	Pd. 1.00.
B. G. Bacon	Pd. 1.00
Leo W. Thacher	Pd. 10.00
Chas. R. Simpkins	Pd 5.00
H.K.	2.00
B. R. Bassett	1.00

E.D. Payne	2.00
A.H. Eldredge	1.00
A. Howland	1.00
R. H. Hall	1.00
W. H. Thacher	1.00
Russell Hallet	1.00
Wang Davis	2.00
Undetermined	
M.G. Myciek	1.00
Jamie Myciek	1.00
Clara W. Sears	1.00
Lewis H. Suow	1.00
G.G. Thacher	1.00
E.B. Hallet	1.00
T. Taylor	.50
Joseph Basset	1.00

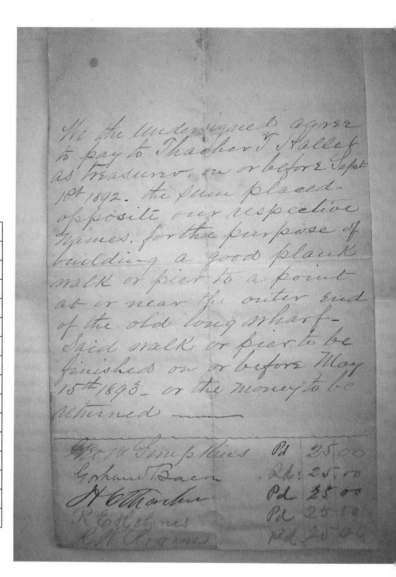

This is a photo of the Bass Hole over the boardwalk at the end in September of 1925. However today, the boardwalk does not cross the channel at the end. In the early 1920s to the 1950s, you could cross the marsh area to the beach at the other side.

Harvesting fresh fish with a pitchfork, these fishermen had to work on both the in and outgoing tides. Their fishing schedule would change based upon the weather and tide. Suited in their work gear, this gives us an image of what a fisherman was. The strenuous work of loading and hauling fish and being on the water attracted a certain type of person.

Repairing and rigging the nets were also part of a fisherman's daily routine. The nets were rigged so when the tide came in they could be lowered to trap the fish. This would coordinate with the in and outgoing tides. As the tide would then go out, the nets would be dropped to catch the fish for the daily harvest. These photographs were provided by William P. Quinn.

Here you can see that the pier was once destroyed. During this time there was no such thing as pressure treated wood or posts driven to 90 feet into the mud, so the tide could easily wipe out the pier. Between wind currents, tides, and ice, it was not uncommon for piers to disintegrate under the mercy of Mother Nature.

The Harwood Palmer stuck off the point of Wharf Lane.

Boston, Mass,

Stranding accident – Schooner Harwood Palmer

She left Boston January 24th, anchoring that night in 29 fathoms of water about seven miles northwest of Cape Cod in a most severe northeast gale of wind. The gale that did so much damage to shipping off our coast. She lay in this position until the next morning when one chain parted. The Captain then managed to get enough sail on to drive her into the lee of Provincetown where she anchored in 14 fathoms of water with her remaining anchor. She lay in this position seven or eight hours when she parted her remaining chain. The Captain then headed her for the most favorable beach he could find and she took bottom during the night of the 25th high up on Yarmouth Beach, Cape Cod Massachusetts.

The beach at this place is almost flat and was at low tide, the bottom being soft sand. The vessel was and is absolutely un-injured. The ice then set in. For five or six weeks the schooner was imprisoned in the ice which was at times more than eight feet thick rendering relief operations impossible. The ice went out on March 10th and by means of seven anchors and half mile hausers from the stern of the vessel she was hauled back from 200 to 300 feet in which position she remained until the next run of high tides just concluded during which she was hauled back 530 measured feet and is now within a matter of 600 to 700 feet from water that will be deep enough to float her at any ordinary high tide. The vessel lies in a dredged channel and we have a dredge now at work directly behind her digging a channel towards deep water.

We hope that the enclosed assessment of $200 per 1/64 will be all that is needed for extracting the vessel from her stranding accident. There are at present on the vessel, bills for about $11,000 and we are not yet through with the expense of dredging. Of this sum $3,500 is for anchor and chains to replace those lost. About $2,000 is for dredge services to date. About $3,000 for hausers and the remainder is made up of crew expenses, provisions, lighterage and incidentals. A detailed statement will be made as soon as the vessel is afloat. In as much as your agent has been obliged to advance much of this money, a prompt remittance will be appreciated.

Respectfully,

April 24, 1905

William F. Palmer

The day Matthews boarded a Five Masted Schooner by William P. Quinn.

On a pleasant Friday afternoon in late September, I had just finished covering a short news story for television news and decided to stop in at Hallet's store in Yarmouthport to deliver some photographs I had made for Matthews Hallet. One of the pictures was of the five-masted schooner Harwood Palmer, one of the famous fleet that operated from the port of Boston. The schooner was aground in the ice in Cape Cod Bay and was stuck there from January 1905 until March 24th 1905. Needless to say with my interest in shipwrecks all around Cape Cod I was keenly interested in the story about the schooner in the ice. As I came into the store, Matthews was at a corner table with a couple of his friends discussing the topics of the day. I brought the photos over and gave them to Matthews and asked him about the vessel in the ice. Matthews with a sly grin told me the story about how a January storm had driven two schooners ashore, one in Dennis, a four master, and the Harwood Palmer in Yarmouthport. When asked about the incident, Matthews said, "Of course, you know I was aboard the Harwood Palmer. One of the friends looked quizzically at Matthews and said: "Why Matthews, you were not born until June 1905, so how could you have been aboard her?" Well Matthews answered with a sly grin on his lips: "Well in early March, Mother and Dad went aboard her and had tea with the Captain. So I was aboard her! Of course I was still in embryo but dammit I was aboard her!"

Overlooking the bay, there are 3 full masted schooners on the horizon. This photo was taken in the late 1800s somewhere off of Cape Cod Bay.

Bombay 25th June 1852

Elisha T. Loring Esqr.
Boston Mass.
U.S.A.

Sir,

We are in receipt of a letter from Truman Hinckley Esqr. so dated 13th April, making enquiry relative to the late Charles L. Stowe, who was unfortunately drowned on this Harbour in December last, while sailing in a Boat in company with the Chief Officer of the "Brig Pansick", who was also drowned, and the notice of the Police was received.

We understand that the young man belonged to the American ship "Race Horse", then here, but being a foreign vessel the authorities did not interfere, and we therefore have been unable to obtain more than general information; we understand that Captain Porter promised to write home full particulars, which he may perhaps have done from China, meantime we learn from the Administrator General that he has no effect of the Deceased in his possession, as you will observe by the enclosed copy of a letter he has addressed to us.

We regret it is not in our power to furnish you with more precise information, but should the "Race Horse" again come here, which is not unlikely, we will make a point of seeing Captain Porter on the subject.

We pass this letter open then that our friends Messrs Forbes Esqr. and with a tender of services remain,

Sir,
Your most obedient servant
Forbes & Co.

Copy ⅌ Steamer of 28th June.

No. 323 of 1852

Estate of Charles Stones deceased.
un administered.

To
Messrs. Forbes & Co.
Bombay

Gentlemen

I have the honor to acknowledge the receipt of your letter of yesterday's date, and you reply to inform you that I have not administered the Estate of the abovenamed deceased, and that I do not hold and am now aware of these being in the Jurisdiction any money or effects belonging thereto.

I have the honor to be
Gentlemen,
Your most obedient servant
Signed Spencer Compton
Administrator General.

Bombay —
Admn? Genls office
the 24th of June 1852

True Copy
F.G.?

29

This glass plate photo is of a painting by R. Spencer. The title reads;
"Martha N. Hail 610 Tons Reg! N. B. Burgess. Com <u>dr</u>
Off Dover. Eng. Chan!"

Another glass plate photograph of a painting by R. Spencer. Banner reads "William S. Hilles," and has an American Flag. It is unknown if these paintings still exist.

The Sandy Neck Lighthouse was the landmark in the 1800s for incoming ships to bring their goods to the wharf off of Wharf Lane into Barnstable Harbor. Over the years the landscape has changed dramatically due to weather and currents, so now in June 2007 replace the missing top and light and currently there is a fundraising effort to restore it.

Sandy Neck Lighthouse
Dimensions and Overview

Old Light List No. 69 (Obsolete)
41° 43'18"N, 70° 16'30"W
Ht. above water 33 feet
10 lamps later Fresnel lens
Built 1827 (tower on house)
Rebuilt 1857 (separate tower)
Range: 11 *miles*
Fixed white light, white tower
Disestablished 1921 (replaced by skeleton tower until 1952)
Privately owned today

Sandy Neck (sometimes called Beach Point) Light is on the tip of the barrier dunes protecting Barnstable harbor and the great marsh behind them. Because Barnstable had a Custom House, shipyards, and heavy traffic of Boston-bound packets and fishermen, Barnstable town meeting ceded two acres to the United States on July 22, 1826. Massachusetts, by act of the General Court, had already ceded four acres (for lights here and at Long Point) on June 20, 1826.

During the next year a brick keeper's house, with a wooden tower on its roof, was built. The light was thirty-three feet above the sea, with ten lamps and reflectors, showing a fixed white light visible for twelve miles. The Congressional appropriation had been $3700.

Few keepers' logs readily reveal the names of keepers. However, some at Sandy Neck are known. There was, for instance, Jacob S. Howes, who married Eunice Crowell. She was a seventh-generation descendant of John Crow, one of the settlers of Yarmouth in 1639. When Jacob died, she became keeper for two years. Thomas Baxter was another keeper; he married Lucy Hinckley, an ancestor of John Crocker (who owns the logs quoted on the following page). These names-Crowell, Baxter, Hinckley, Crocker all fill numerous pages of today's Cape Cod telephone books.

The elements took their toll of the Sandy Neck Light Station. By 1857 the house with its roof tower had to be demolished, and the current brick tower, painted white, was built, with a new Victorian keeper's house. An unusual feature of the construction of the house was insertion of brick walls between the studs of the frame. As a result the house is warm in winter and cool in summer. The tower is still there and though the lantern has been removed and the tower capped. It showed a fixed white light. But well before World War II, in 1931 the lighthouse was disestablished because of large accessions of sand to the tip of Sandy Neck. The optic was moved from the old tower to a steel skeleton tower some two hundred feet closer to the tip. An automatic acetylene light (like those used on large buoys at that time) was installed but was shown only from April to October. During World War II the Coast Guard used the station as a beach patrol headquarters.

In 1952 this light also was discontinued, and the property was declared surplus on June 12, 1953. Edward B. Hinckley and his wife, on December 4, 1954, bought the house and tower for $1551. Their daughter, Lois Hinckley, owns it today.

So ends the story of Sandy Neck Lighthouse and its keepers, who for 104 years served the needs of the port of Barnstable. Although the port is still active, most of the vessels are pleasure craft, with a few fishermen, and not the working sloops and schooners of the old days.

One of the early keepers was Captain Henry Baxter, who kept the light from 1833 to 1844, after a long career in the coastwise trade. His first log entry on relieving Joseph Nickerson, the first keeper, read: *"This day moved my family and took possession of the light house at Beach Point, Sandy neck, Wind NE, Thick weather."* This was on Sunday, December 1, 1833. Other entries reveal some of the problems a keeper faced:

12/15/34: *This day a heavy gale from the SW with snow. Came on shore the schooner Enterprise of Mount ? and Capt. Sawyer with two women on board. Got them on shore with much trouble. Capt. Sawyer much frostbit. So ends very cold and the ice making fast the schooner....*

On January 6, 1835, another schooner stranded near the light. His log recorded: *"Extream cold most emposable to keep the oil with a lens in the lanton all the time."* It was a rugged winter. On February 8 he notes: *". . . the harbor all shut up with ice. The water out of both wells-not able to get any water out of eather."*

His final entry for 1835 was: *So ends this year ... there being 650 schooners and 361 sloops and 2 brigs that has passed in and out over the bar (his yearly report of vessels passing). Schooner Globe made 33 trips, Sappho 35 trips to Boston.*

Another entry notes that a March storm "washed away the bank to the South end of the lighthouse about 70 feet."

Lieutenant Carpender had this to say during his inspection of the light station in 1838: *This light is on a low, sandy point at the entrance to the harbor, elevated 25 feet [Other sources say 33 or (later) 44feet.] above the level of the sea. [Of the ten lamps] I recommended suppression of the upper tier. It cannot be that this light requires more lamps than either of the Plymouth (Plymouth-the Gurnet-had two lighthouses at that time.]*

He continues, pointing out that having a wooden tower on a brick house "*is an exceedingly injudicious arrangement, for, if any accident from fire happens to either, both are liable to be destroyed.... The premises here are in good order.*"

In 1887 the Lighthouse Board reported that: *The brick tower, being badly cracked, was strengthened with two iron hoops and six staves. The wooden bulkhead was extensively repaired and filled with sand, and minor repairs were made.*

Taken from *Lighthouses of Cape Cod-Martha's Vineyard-Nantucket: Their History and Lore* by Admont G. Clark

This is the Mill Pond Area showing Mill Lane heading toward Mill Bridge. On the left is a group of local residents ice fishing.

Mill Bridge is a division between Barnstable and Yarmouth. As the photo shows, this is the Barnstable side and it seems as if the daily chores of bringing water for the workmen at this Fish Shanty had just occurred. The incoming tide changes in this area between four and five feet, and this picture was taken on an outgoing tide and a lot of the shoreline workers worked according to the tide change. Workmen were at the mercy of the in and out coming tides.

Mill Bridge and Lovell's Fish Shanty on the north side of the bridge on the Barnstable side.

This picture was taken from the wharf on Wharf Lane looking toward the Congregational Church. As you view the landscape, very little trees existed across the marsh and shoreline, so the houses were very prominent.

This steam powered mobile rock crusher located on Vesper Lane in Yarmouth, crushed several tons of rock for the Old Kings Highway, also known as 6A. In 1892, Andrew Hallet was Highway Commissioner and hundreds of weight slips he signed can be found in the Hallet Museum. These may show the process of when they were putting the stone along Old Kings Highway.

A rare look into early road construction equipment

In the late 1800s and early 1900s, steamrollers were used to set the crushed rock into the roads. As tons of crushed rocks were hauled up off Vesper Lane, this steamroller set base of crushed rocks along 6A. This was the first hard service for the scenic road.

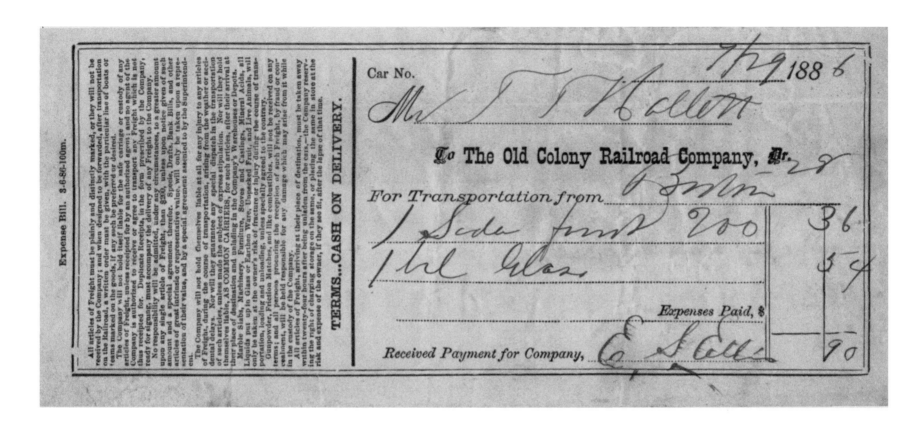

From the Chatham Celebration, 1712-1912   C-1913

RAILROADS AND OTHER PUBLIC MEANS OF TRAVEL.   Page 49: Early Conditions. Excerpts….

     Communication with Boston was at first a matter of considerable time and discomfort. The journey could be made on horseback, or advantage could be taken of the casual vessels that made the voyage the Chatham to that port. The fishing vessels in the fall frequently took the dried fish there for sale and returned with provisions and goods to supply the winter needs of the inhabitants. Around 1830, packets were run from Brewster and Chatham to Boston. Some of us can remember the Chatham packets at the wharf of Josiah Hardy near the Lights and the ball and flag on the former doctor's house on the north road that indicated the sailing and arrival of the Brewster packet. Much use of this was made by the Chatham people to avoid the trip around the Cape. The railroad was completed to Sandwich in 1848. Lines of stages were then run from Chatham to Yarmouth and at one time there was a line also to Hyannis. In 1865 Harwich was reached by the railroad and from that time on a short carriage ride was required until the Chatham railroad was opened in 1887.

Dennis

This schoolhouse and church are located in Dennis. This photo was taken in the early 1900s.

The Nobscussett House on Cape Cod Bay in Dennis. The great depression of the 30s caused the house to be dismantled in 1934, but it once consisted of 215 acres of land, three cottages, a bowling alley, a horse stable, a billiard room, and a golf course. Adjacent to the hotel stood two Nobscussett cottages. In the top right you see an invitation to a Ball in September of 1889 celebrating the 250th Anniversary of the founding of Old Yarmouth. Also on the top left is an actual ribbon you would receive if you attended the Ball.

These were the guesthouse cottages to the Nobscussett House. The cottages were of a high-class upscale region, where as you can see from this photo, these were no ordinary cottages and were the finest places to stay on Cape Cod as they coincide with the prestige of the Nobscussett House.

❖NOBSCUSSETT HOUSE,❖

DENNIS, (CAPE COD) MASS.

FRANK B. TOBEY, (of Chicago,) Owner and Prop.

THIS POPULAR SUMMER HOME

Enjoys many attractions peculiar to itself.

A BEAUTIFUL, ELEVATED LOCATION,

Every outlook from which recalls some incident of the early occupation by the Pilgrims or of their peaceful neighbors the Nobscussett Indians.

QUIET AND RESTFUL SECLUSION

From the wear of work-a-day life is secured by the 180 acres belonging to the estate.

PURE SEA AIR with PERFECT SANITATION

Insures the Absence of Malaria, Hay Fever and kindred troubles.

AN ABUNDANT SUPPLY OF SPRING WATER,

Which analysis proves "*Purer* than even the famed *Poland Sping Water.*"

Miles of Unsurpassed Bathing Beaches, Excellent Boating and Fishing, invite to the more active pleasures of Seaside Holiday Life.

For Illustrated Book, Letters from well-known Guests, Terms, &c., address

F. H. PRATT, Manager,

DENNIS, MASS.

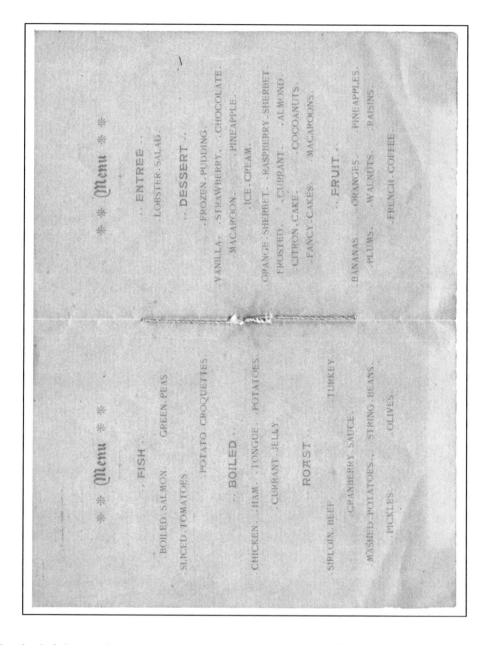

On the left is an advertisement in the 1895 Directory of Barnstable, Yarmouth, and Dennis, and on the right is an actual menu from 1889 Celebration Ball of the 250th Anniversary of the founding of Old Yarmouth held at the Nobscussett House. I recommend the chicken.

On the left is the Jacob Sears Library on Old Main Street in East Dennis. This is the typical canopy-like traveled way, as the trees overshadowed the old roadways.

Yarmouth Village

This home was located on Old Kings Highway near Weir Road and belonged to Rebecca Sturgis. It was given to her by the town due to the loss of her home by fire and is believed to have been demolished in 1918.

Located at 477 Main Street in Yarmouth, this house belonged to the Hedge Family in the early 1800s. At one point it was a stagecoach stop. It was also once McAbee Real Estate and is now a co-op of office building. It sits on the corner of Union Street and 6A.

This house is on 450 Old Kings Highway at the end of West Yarmouth Road on 6A in Yarmouth and is on the left side of the park. It was a built in 1721 where it was originally a private residence. Later it would become a tavern during the late 1700s, but it eventually would become a residence again.

On 438 Old Kings Highway in Yarmouthport, Alfred Thacher built this house in 1840. George Hallet II also lived here in the late 1880s to the early 1900s. Today it is the Blueberry Manor.

On 189 Center Street in Yarmouth, this home originally belonged to Andrew Hedge Eldridge in the mid 1800s. As you make your way to the boardwalk at the Bass Hole, the homes surrounding the marshland were of well-known families.

In Yarmouth on 431 Old Kings Highway, this house is believed to have been built in 1750. It was Gilpin's Antique's for many years and is directly across from Center Street. The family in the photo is believed to be the Ryder family who lived in the home during the late 1880s and early 1900s.

Located at 399 Old Kings Highway, this house belonged to Captain Gorham Howland in the mid to late 1800s. Also living here were the Clark family, and Mr. and Mrs. William Sherman in the mid 1900s. There is an attached garage and office.

Located at 381 Old Kings Highway in Yarmouthport, this house belonged to Captain Ezra Howes in the late 1880s. This home is at the corner of Pine Street and 6A and is hidden by a 6-foot hedge that replaced one of the beautiful fences from the 1800s.

This house was built around the 1800s for Captain Oliver Gorham at 364 Old Kings Highway in Yarmouth. In this early 1900s photograph we see members of Oliver Gorham's family. Today it is next to the *Barn & Co.* in Yarmouth. From the detail moldings of the porch, to a picket fence, to an access way on the right side, to the barn in the back, all are unique characteristics for a house of this period.

Other members of the Gorham family lived in this house, which is located at 361 Old Kings Highway right next to the Friday Club. It also once belonged to Tom Baker. It was very common for homes to have three chimneys and for families to pose when their homes were photographed during the late 1800s.

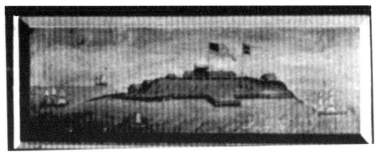

There is one of seven of these glass plate photographs of the interior of a unique Cape Cod fireplace. The paintings above the fireplace portrayed sea captains' lives. They showed ships coming and going, landscape scenes, and portraits (all seen on the left). The location of this David Thacher home.

Here, Edmund Walker, a local wood merchant poses by his wagon loaded with firewood. His job is ongoing since firewood was always in demand and was a very lucrative business. However wood was not the only source of fuel for the stoves of that time. Coal and kerosene would eventually become more popular much to the dismay of Mr. Walker.

Here's another shot of Edmund Walker storing firewood for another winter.

THE NEW HUB RANGE

The Patent Wire Gauze Oven Door
IS THE LATEST IMPROVEMENT ON
THE NEW HUB RANGE.

READ THESE IMPORTANT FACTS!

The Wire Gauze Door *does not cool the oven*.

The Wire Gauze Door *does not require extra fuel*, because the fresh air which is admitted, is constantly combining with the carbon in the meat or bread, thus producing extra heat, and actually requiring much less fuel than with the close door.

The Wire Gauze Oven Door makes meat tender and palatable.

The Wire Gauze Oven Door prevents the shrinkage of the meat, or the evaporation of its juices. The fresh oxygen entering the oven closes the cells of the meat, thus preventing the escape of the juices.

The Wire Gauze Oven Door roasts meats as perfectly as they can be roasted before the fire or on a spit.

The Wire Gauze Oven Door produces larger loaves of bread that are more healthful and nutritious than can be obtained from any other oven.

The Wire Gauze Oven Door bakes pastry to perfection. Cake, pies and fancy pastry of every description are cooked uniformly on every side, and the top cannot be distinguished from the bottom.

The Wire Gauze Oven Door does not throw off bad odors into the room, as the fresh air entering the oven neutralizes all odors and prevents their escape.

The Wire Gauze Oven Door enables cooking to be done with the oven at 100 degrees lower temperature than the ordinary range, thus diminishing the wear and tear of the range. Read our complete circular for additional facts.

SMITH & ANTHONY STOVE CO.,
MANUFACTURERS,
52 & 54 UNION ST., BOSTON, MASS.
4-51

Everyone had an icebox in the days before refrigerators, so here you see local residents cutting ice on Dennis pond on the Willow Street side of the pond.

Dennis Pond looking towards Willow Street.

If you've ever had a chance to walk around the pond, you can tell the small inlets in the rocky formation on one side, and the smooth formation on the other side. This pond is spring fed by old abandoned cranberry bogs. Before Willow Street and the railroad bridge was built, several ponds interconnected through underground streams.

This is the North side of Dennis Pond, toward Summer Street. It had two icehouses, one on each end. This end of the pond had an old bog attached that was fed by an underground stream.

Old Yarmouth Brass Band around the late 1880s, but only nine out of the thirteen members can be identified. From left to right the band members are; unknown, Alfred Howland, unknown, Harry Ryder, Carlton Ryder, Elmer Hallet, Bill Cahoon, N.T. Hallet, John Brice, Herb Vincent, unknown, Charles Swift, and unknown.

The Sacred Heart Chapel was built in 1899. Today this church is being used in spilt sessions due to overcrowding and lack of parking space because during its origin, there were only a handful of Catholics living in Yarmouth and a large church was not necessary. Services were only held during the summer, where a visiting priest from Falmouth held Mass at Lyceum Hall or another worshipper's home.

This is a late 1800s photograph of the inside of the First Congregational Church of Yarmouth. It sits on top of a hill on the border of Yarmouth and Yarmouthport, and is probably one of the highest points in Yarmouthport. This is only one of four churches in Yarmouthport, but all support different faiths. Notice the pipe organ and the gas lamps.

The families that settled in Yarmouth had their values instilled in them by their faith. Regardless of what faith you practice, you realize that all religions helped to endure hardships. Births and deaths were recorded in books of their faith, which left a deep record of family history. As families pass these bibles along to their children, some have kept their ancestors informed of their heritage on the Cape. Roots go deep and some records are only kept in these books, and as we know religion played a big role as they sought guidance from their churches. You can tell by the number of churches in Barnstable, Dennis, and Yarmouth of how truly important religion was to the early settlers.

In the bible of Daniel Taylor, the particular detail they used to enter the record keeping to the Matthews C. Hallet book is hard to interpret. From the use of quill pens to the pencil, the way the information was recorded varied. Family members realized their effort was not in vain.

This home belonged to Everett Bray, and was moved to Yarmouth atop of a hill along side the First Congregational Church as the ditty box.

Flames consume this Unitarian Church that was once was located in Barnstable. It looks like it was surrounded by an iron fence and monuments, which may indicate a cemetery. What is also unique is the rooster weathervane on top of the steeple.

Windmills

This is a photo of some children playing by the abandoned windmill in Yarmouth. As the Cape from coast to coast abandoned its windmills, wind farms (a new technology) started to take their place. Regardless of what century you live in, wind power is still a major source of energy. As these huge new windmills dot the skyline at three to four times the height of the old ones and generate electricity for the community, the Cape Cod citizens highly opposed the new means of technology. These windmills block the ocean view as they are set on horizon of our ocean line as opposed to the shoreline, where the old mills once stood.

The old windmills, if they weren't pumping seawater for the saltworks, they were grinding corn for your cornbread. They would also be pumping water for your drinking water. However these new mills purely generate electricity.

Yarmouth Gristmill was believed to be in back of the Friday Club at one point. By the looks of its condition, this mill was abandoned for many years. This glass-plate photo was taken in the late 1800s.

Hanover Square at the Yarmouth Methodist Campground is off of Willow Street. During the 1800s, this was a major meeting place for local residents to come and worship at the camp's tabernacle and cottages, and a large majority came from outside Yarmouth as well. Unfortunately the tabernacle was destroyed in 1944 by a hurricane and over the years the campground area has become more of a summer home and the cottages have been renovated. The Methodist camp meetings stopped in 1946 and today this area is mostly used during the summer for vacationers.

The right side of this building was a post office in Hanover Square on the Yarmouth Methodist Campground.

Here the Cook and Greenough families pose with their wagon on Summer Street, formally Hawes Lane, in Yarmouthport. As we all know, from sunrise to sunset everyone had their weight to pull…including the dog.

This is the interior of the sitting room in the Aiken family home. You can tell the Aiken family was wealthy from the wide format of the banister railing, the prominent structure of the fireplace, the elegant detail of the wall covering, the carpet like material that lies beneath the three hand-woven rugs, the mantel on top of the fireplace and the silverback mirror above it.

Early Transportation

and

Roadways

May Russell Howes Thacher.

In this era, this was a common site as this was the only means of travel to bring back goods to their homes and businesses.

Here we see Pat Hannon driving his carriage past Hallet's store heading toward Dennis in 1905.
I guess you can say this carriage has two-horse power.

This is at the curve in the road at Summer Street and Old Kings Highway in Yarmouthport. When you would be standing at the pump at this corner, the Yarmouth Inn would be on your right, and the Parnassus Bookstore would be on your left. The building on your right does not exist anymore. It was the original home of the *Yarmouth Register* newspaper and a meat market.

Old Kings Highway in Yarmouth.

At the corner of Union Street looking east, these houses (numbers 496, 500, 502) would be on your left as you rode your horse towards Provincetown. These houses are the typical Cape style homes, and if you notice the trees are not fully developed to take the road over yet.

In Yarmouth, this is Old Kings Highway going east, just before Center Street on the left. The house number on your left would be 424 and the one on your right would be 425.

In Yarmouthport standing on Old Kings Highway by Gingerbread Lane looking west, on your left would be the two banks, Bank of America and Cape Cod Cooperative Bank. The house that is on your left in this glass-plate was either torn down or moved. Notice the canopies of the trees that have now engulfed the road. Also take notice of the rings around the trees, as this was a tar-like substance that was applied to prevent caterpillars from climbing the trees to eat the leaves. These caterpillars would make cocoons that would look like a tent in the tree.

Old Kings Highway, also known as 6A and Hallet Street in Yarmouthport

You're on your horse in front of Hallet's store, you're riding east and on the right side peeking between the trees is the roofline of the Town Crier. As you travel east, the beautiful canopy of trees keeps you shaded from the hot sweltering sun on your destination back home with a mustard plaster pack that you picked up from T.T. Hallet's drugstore.

Going East on Old Kings Highway, as you got out of your wagon and tied your horse to a granite post, you then go into Hallet's store (on the right) to mail a letter, since Hallet's was then used as a post office.

The curve at the road in Yarmouthport, Old Kings Highway after the pump going west, on your right-hand side is the building before Lyceum Hall. On your left the house is 201 Old Kings Highway.

Going west on 149 Old Kings Highway, Fred Grobe's house is on your right and Hallet's store is to the left.

Old Kings Highway Sandy Side Lane

This is between Hallet's store and the Cancer Shop and was the entranceway to the estate of the Honorable John Simpkins, a Massachusetts Senator during the late 1800s. He died at a young age from a sudden illness and in his memory the John Simpkins High School was built, as he was also the head of the education department.

"SANDY SIDE."
LATE RESIDENCE OF MRS. JOHN SIMPKINS
YARMOUTH PORT MASS.

Senator John Simpkins

The John Simpkins Estate (left) was built by John Simpkin's mother upon the death of his father. As the entrance of Sandy Side was widened, the rock wall pillars were disassembled, where it went from a private estate to being used for residential homes. The main estate resides as a home today and is situated at the end of Sandy Side Lane overlooking Dennis Pond. Before the trees overtook Dennis Pond, there was a beautiful view of it from the estate. Simpkins' office resided on the second floor of Hallet's store in the front. Many old senate pictures were hung up on the walls where he worked. He achieved many great things at such a young age from being a Massachusetts Senator to being the head of the Education Department. Also before he died, documents of naval intervention and rescue were things he had been working on.

Charles Warren Hallet
Oliver Hallet

Story told by Lois Hallet Betterley

Lois Betterley is a descendent of Oliver Hallet. She grew up in Barnstable where she spent her childhood in the Barnstable-Cummaquid area. As she recalls her past…

This portion of the Hallet family history is derived through the ancestors of Andrew Hallet. Charles of Hallet's Store and my common ancestor was our great great great grandfather, Captain Ancel Hallet. His sons Ancel Jr. and Edward married sisters Charlotte and Rebecca. Thus Charles and our side of the family are many times removed, but we are cousins nonetheless.

My grandfather was Charles Warren Hallet. He had an upholster shop beside his Cummaquid 6A home. He was a navy man who served aboard the battleship *Oklahoma*. His two sons Francis and George were aboard at the same time. Charles worked in the engine room, while his sons served as sailors. This ship later was sunk at Pearl Harbor. He had many stories of his sea life and the local teen boys would ride their bikes to his home and gather for his tales.

Pete Howland and the Philbrook boy had their bikes run over in the driveway one day by Charles' "Little Green Hornet" car, as he backed up onto 6A. Charles was famous for driving to the Cummaquid post-office, coming out and walking home, only to think his car had been stolen.

Charles also loved conventions. He attended every convention for veterans of foreign wars, as he was also a veteran of the Spanish-American War, as well as a navy man. When he died in 1945, we grandchildren were given our share of his service medals and medal like mementos of these conventions, which are still somewhere in the Cummaquid house now owned by my daughter and son-in-law, Charlene and Peter Smith. Five generations of our family have been raised in that house.

Charles was a character, and the Boston Herald once ran a cartoon of him in their newspaper. He had a hearing aid and was deaf as ever. Back in the 40s, we had a minister from the Unitarian Church who used to visit the families now and again. Of course Charles was in his shop cussing away and did not hear the minister upon his arrival, quite embarrassing for his daughter Alice, who lived with my grandfather.

Charles used to plow up the whole backyard and grow a wonderful array of fruits and vegetables. We as children, living across the field on Mary Dunn Road, used to raid his melon patch. Of course he knew, but he never said anything.

I know also he used to make a great Quahog chowder for the Barnstable County Fair, then located on 6A at the Old Fair Grounds in Barnstable.

Charles in his younger days used to travel to Boston and drive the new cars home for the rich and elite of Osterville and Hyannis port. He was very mechanical and also kept the cars in running order.

Jessie Hallet, Charles' oldest child, lived over 100 years. She married Winslow Knowles Thacher, an older local man who had gone west. He was a stagecoach driver in the 1880's. They say Winslow, Arizona was named after him. Jessie was an independent woman for the early 1900's. She was the first woman ambulance driver in Boston.

Charles' older boys were typical boys. Jessie being the older sister was always trying to prevent their punishment. For instance, they attended the Unitarian Church, and after everyone was seated, down the aisle came George and Francis chasing a pig. My father was one of Charles' younger children. He was a golf pro at the Cummaquid golf course. He died quite young in 1964. He was named after his grandfather Oliver.

Oliver Hallet and Maria Catherine Elizabeth Lashbrook were my father's grandfather and grandmother. The son of Edward and Rebecca Hallet, Oliver Hallet is a descendent of Andrew Hallet who in 1639, was one of the first comers to Yarmouth. He was born on the Hallet family farm on Wharf Lane in Yarmouthport. Oliver had four brothers; Warren, Charles, Edward, and George.

Coming from a seafaring family, Oliver turned to the sea at an early age. He first went to sea when he was about twelve or thirteen. Around the same age he was aboard the clipper ship, "Tornado," which made a record-breaking trip from New York to San Francisco. When he was 25, he was about to get his papers ready to become a captain, however the Civil War was soon to break. In 1861, he enlisted in the U.S. Navy as an Acting Masters Mate on the U.S.S. Fear Not.

In about 1857, Oliver was on board a clipper ship working under the command of Captain Freeman of Wellfleet, Massachusetts. The ship was docked at a port in Australia where another ship from England was docked as well. It was from that ship where Oliver met Maria Catherine Elizabeth Lashbrook, the niece of a doctor aboard the ship. Maria went by many names, most commonly Elizabeth. Elizabeth was also an orphan who was unhappy with her home life. Captain Freeman and his wife had no children, and with Elizabeth's uncle knowing of her unhappiness, the Captain was given permission to adopt Elizabeth since he could provide a better life. Now with Oliver and Elizabeth aboard the same ship, he began his courtship of her and they would be married in 1860.

Oliver and Elizabeth lived in their house on Wharf Lane all of their lives where they had seven children; Charles Warren, Grace E., Alice C., Georgie Lashbrook, Edward Pulsifer, Oliver Jr., and Marian R. However in February of 1911, there was a heavy blizzard. Oliver had left the house to go to the barn, and while he was making his way back to his house, the storm became too much for him. The blizzard blinded him so that he became lost and would fall and hit his head, falling into the snow. Elizabeth became worried when her husband did not return and sent Edward out to look for him, where he found him covered in snow. Despite bring him back into the house where they wrapped him in blankets and putting his feet in warm water, Oliver would develop pneumonia and died shortly after.

Oliver Hallet was not only a seafaring man, a naval officer, but a farmer as well. He experimented with soil and successfully crossbred a Japanese Plum Tree with another fruit tree. He also helped plant the Elm Trees on Hallet Street that you see in the photograph collection of Matthews C. Hallet. These trees grew to be a beautiful canopy over 6A, which have become a trademark of these old photographs. As one the ancestors of the Hallet namesake, Oliver was one of the main family members who pioneered the sections of Barnstable, Yarmouth and Cummaquid.

Information provided by Barbara Hallett-Beaupre

The West Dennis side of Bass River.

The windmill in the distance is still there to this day and boathouses dot the shoreline. Bass River is an inlet for the south side of the Cape. It travels all the way up and through Follins Pond.

This is the Dennis side of Bass River in Yarmouth. In the foreground there is a dismasted and abandoned hull that served as a pier for catboats, which were the sport craft of the 19th century. The coal schooner, *David K. Akin* is sitting on the opposite bank moored with a headsail raised. Tied in front of the waterfront store, you can see another coastal schooner.

Here are two anchor draggers moored near the Bass River Bridge on the Dennis side of the river. The Bass River Bridge was once a toll bridge that connected Dennis and Yarmouth. Bass River is one of the villages in Yarmouth.

This small area shows the Saltworks near Mill Pond in Yarmouthport. This was located near the Mill Bridge area where it used the inlet that filled Mill Pond from Cape Cod Bay. The area was an ideal location due to the higher ground and the water-fed inlet, which made it have easier access to saltwater, so it did not always have to be pumped as far.

This map of Mill Pond shows the small working saltworks and the various inlets. This area is where Mill Bridge connects with Yarmouthport and Barnstable.

Located in Barnstable, this is a long view of the Loring Crocker saltworks. This view was most likely taken from across the creek as shown on the map on the following page.

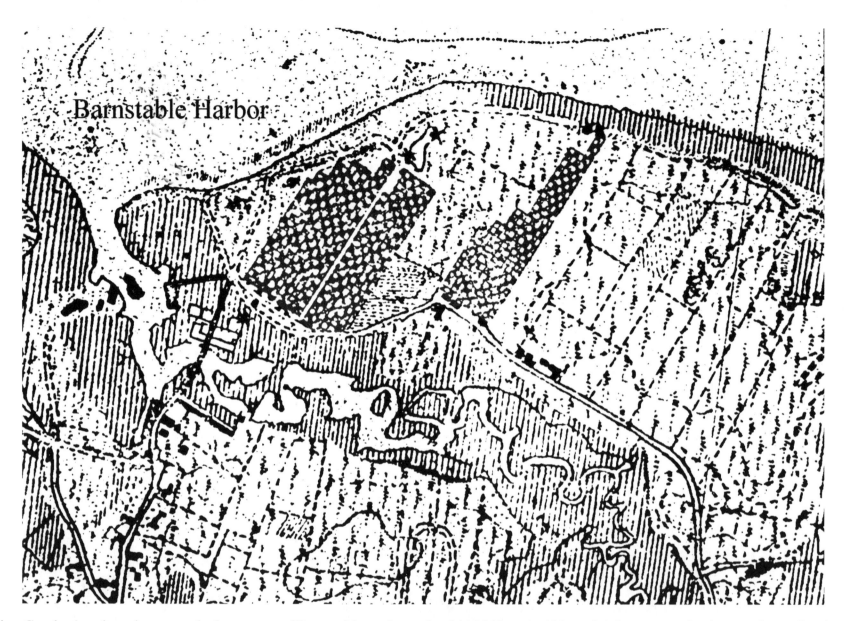

Loring Crocker's saltworks covered a large area of Barnstable as shown by this 1849 map. Although it is not exactly shown where, Crocker had a cannon mounted in 1814 to protect his saltworks. It was most likely located near the shoreline. The largest town on the Cape is Barnstable, located in the central part of the peninsula and running from Cape Cod Bay to the Nantucket Sound. It is the shire town of Barnstable County. Loring Crocker had his saltworks on the common fields at Barnstable Village. The tax lists showed that in 1831 there were 920,750 superficial feet of saltworks here. In 1841 the number came down slightly to 876,450. In 1850 the saltworks had begun their decline and the number was 94,000.

The saltwork maps and the following excerpt are from *The Saltworks of Historic Cape Cod* by William P. Quinn.

The owners of the saltworks were listed in Deyo's History:

"Nathaniel Gorham boiled sea water and made salt, on Sandy Neck, during the revolutionary war. Many of the present residents of Barnstable village remember when the "Common Field" - the marsh in the rear of the Unitarian church - was a field of salt works. Loring Crocker, grandfather of Alfred Crocker, was the pioneer in this industry on the common field. In 1804 he bought of Isaac Bacon several acres of land with the right to the salt water and the privilege of placing pumps. He afterward, in 1832, bought sixteen hundred running feet of Samuel Whitman, who had succeeded Lothrup Tucker; then east of this he purchased in 1836, works of Mrs. Sturgis; and he bought Asa Young's works, so that when Loring Crocker died, in the fall of 1843, he was the owner of seventeen thousand running feet of vats, most of which were on the Common field.

"After Loring Crocker died, his sons, Nathan and Loring operated the works up to 1856. Loring bought out his brother and operated them until 1872. Loring was the father of Alfred Crocker of Barnstable who worked on the family saltworks.

"Other owners: Nathaniel Gorham; Amos Otis; William Dixon; Henry L. Hopkins who sold to Alvin Howes who sold to Truman D. Eldredge.

"Osterville: owners were: Thomas Ames; Seth Goodspeed, Ebenezer Scudder, George Hinckley; Jacob Lovell had works near O.D. Lovell's boat house, first from the eastward; he used two wind mills to pump the water to the works. Henry Lovell's was next west, then came Deacon Scudder's then George Lovell's.

"Hyannis: During the war of 1812 salt was a prominent industry. Alvin Snow, Henry and Joshua Hallett had extensive works where is now the Sears lumber yard; A.W. Lovell manufactured near the present lumberyard of B.F. Crocker & Co. This like most of the works, was discontinued about 1831. Lot Crocker had works where his descendants now reside, and Ebenezer Bacon's were adjoining. Zenas Gage engaged in the manufacture near his wharf; Simeon Freeman had works at Dunbar Point, and Zenas D. Bassett and Warren Hallett had their works next west. Other manufacturers were Elnathan Lewis, Warren and David Hinckley, and Gorham Lovell.

"Hyannisport: Frederick Scudder, David Hinckley, Deacon James Marchant and Freeman Marchant made salt here soon after 1800."

There were several Barnstable packets. In the early 1800's, the schooner *Comet*, was running from Barnstable to Boston. The sloop *Independence* also ran here and was burned by the British during the War of 1812. There were four well-known packets that ran after the war, the schooners *Globe, Volant, Sappho and Flavilla*, were all built in Barnstable as was the sloop *Freedom*. Other sloops engaged in service were the *Science, James Lawrence, Velocity* and *Mail*. A couple of steamboats were running from Barnstable in the 1840's. The Express and the *Yacht* made regular trips to Boston. The sailing packets did not fade away entirely when the steamboats began running.

As cranberry picking today is automated through floating and knocking them lose, the old method required many laborers with a lot of manpower as the gross would be hand-harvested. The hand-harvested method involved setting strings and creating rows and it would be up to the individual in that row to pick the cranberries completely. In this picture, the cranberries were harvested and put in wooden barrels, and in the later days they would eventually be put in wooden boxes. On the next page you will see how T.T. paid for the work provided on the cranberry bogs.

This document above reads:

T.T. Hallett To Mary Lack
For weeding Cranberry Bog twice during the summer of 1882, the sum of $5.00. Received payment Nov 27th 1882   M.L.

To J. Lack for hoeing and clearing out ditches. $2.00. Received payment. Nov 27th 1882   J. Lack

103

Yarmouthport Village

Anthony Thacher, one of the original settlers in Yarmouthport, built this home for John Thacher located on 240 Old Kings Highway near the corner of Thacher Street and Thacher Shore Road in 1664. It would later become the Society for the Preservation of New England Antiquities. This would be the beginning of where Hallet Street starts going toward the Barnstable-Cummaquid line.

This photograph of David Thacher's home was taken in 1890 and was located on Church Street near Thacher Shore Road. Thatcher lived in this house until his death in 1800, when it was given to his son, David Thatcher Jr. Aside from the trees along the roadside, this house was basically an open field. That entire open field was perfect for farmland.

Standing on 223 Old Kings Highway, the Old Yarmouth Inn was once a tavern and a stagecoach stop. This structure has gone through many renovations, from adding a large parking lot, a kitchen, and a dining facility. This photo shows it as more of a home rather than the business it is today.

In the early 1900s this fork in the road shows Summer Street, formally Hawes Lane, on your right where it is adjacent to Route 6A, also known as Hallet Street. On the left is the Old Yarmouth Inn, and on the right is the Parnassus Bookstore, and straight ahead is the pump, but is not present in this particular glass plate photo. This photograph was taken over 95 years ago.

Sears Manor around late 1800s. This home has been renovated several times over the coarse of the years. This was the home of Joshua Sears and became a noted hotel of Joshua and his brother Charles, which was aptly named the Sears Hotel.

When horsepower actually meant the use of real horses, Kilburn M. Taylor owned this local Carriage Maker and Painter, as the sign in the picture reads. Located in Yarmouthport on 194 Old Kings Highway, Taylor also dealt with other works. The sign over the front door (right) says: "Ready Made Coffins & Caskets." Built around 1800, this Georgian-style house was a shop run by Taylor, the local wheelwright and undertaker. Then in 1911 Benjamin Gorham bought it and opened up a shoe and men's furnishings store. It was then turned into a post office after Gorham moved down the street, and still even later it became home for a local newspaper, *The Yarmouth Register*. After that it then became *Cape Cod Impressions, Inc*, until the late 1980s when it then turned into a Ross Jolly Reality for a limited time, then rented to sell paintings, and finally as it stands today it is a child's boutique.

This building on Old Kings Highway, known as Arthur Connelly's general store, was renovated with an addition on the right side and became the Register Press and after that was used as office space and is now known as a doctor's office.

As the fire is prepared and the wares are set in the cabinet, the daily duties are now done and ready for patrons. This was H.C. Thacher's house, which was a teahouse. It then became the Nickerson home. Nickerson Antique's was in business for years as one of the finest antique shops on Cape Cod. This home was also attached to Thacher Shore Road off the backside and could be accessed from Flintlock Way.

Decorated in bunting and banners for the 250th Anniversary of the town, Daniel Crocker Jr.'s house had a unique rod iron fence that distinguished the era. Blacksmiths were hard at work making these fences. Crocker's father, Daniel Crocker Sr. who ran the country store on the right, built this house. The interior has been changed many times throughout the years, but the exterior has remained virtually the same as it did during the mid 1800s.

The house on the right you will see the Daniel Crocker house that is now used as business office. Located at 159 Old Kings Highway in Yarmouthport, it was the *Emporium* and is now *Design Works*. The cards above read: "Compliments of Daniel B. Crocker & Co., Agents for the 'American Sewing Machine,' Yarmouthport, Mass". To the right of this building was N.T. Hallet's home that became *La Cipollina* and today is the Japanese restaurant, *Inaho*.

Located on 157 Old Kings Highway in Yarmouthport, N.T. Hallet owned the house on the left in the late 1800s. It would later become *La Cipollina Restaurante* and is now *Inaho*, a Japanese restaurant. The house on the right is known as the Town Crier and an antique shop. It also was the Yarmouth Port Post Office, as indicated on the sign above the door by the bike.

This is another photo of the *Inaho* restaurant and Town Crier on Old Kings Highway in Yarmouthport. At the center of Yarmouthport, as you brought your horse and buggy up, the granite posts were designated to where you "parked" your horse. The fences, some of which were of great detail, kept the horses out of the front yards.

This was to right of the Town Crier in the lot that is now vacant, where it would have been three buildings down from Hallet's Store. This house was moved from this location across the street to 146 Old Kings Highway in Yarmouthport. It is now the home of Fred Grobe.

Here is another view of house number 146 on Old Kings Highway in Yarmouthport. The Chinese lanterns and the large welcome sign indicate that someone of vast importance was arriving.

141 and 139 Main Street in Yarmouthport, both owned by the Hallet family.

Matt and Mary Hallet lived on the third floor of 141 at a very young age until they had their daughter Mary. In 1937 they moved to the "Hallet House" at 137 Main Street. 141 was a hardware store, then a beer store, then an art gallery, and now it is a design shop. However Hallet's store at 139, has remained the same aside from the upstairs. It was a meeting room, a library, a Massachusetts senator's office, and still remains intact, but as a museum.

119

This was Charles Swift's home. He was publisher and editor of *The Register*. The Swift family published and edited many historical books in the late 1800s. The house has a Mansard style roof that was shingled, and the top part of the roof was asphalt. This home was eloquent in design by way of the wraparound front porch and the stained glass windows above the entranceways. There was a Cupola attached the roof on the barn. It also had a beautiful view of the water in the mid 1800s.

This "Gingerbread house" is located on 134 Old Kings Highway. This example of a Gothic Revival house has been renovated and has no longer the unique characteristics of the barn board siding and open-end wings. The barn behind it burned down and an addition was put in its place. What was once a residence is now a place of business.

Shoveling Old Kings Highway across from the First National Bank of Yarmouth.

Formed in 1864, the First National Bank of Yarmouth was originally built in 1825, when it was the Bank of Barnstable. This building was eventually demolished, and the bank location was moved to a new location right next door. It would remain the First National Bank of Yarmouth until the 1970s when it was bought out by the Bank of Boston, which would then be taken over by Fleet Bank. However today it stands as Bank of America, which is next to the Cape Cod Cooperative Bank.

No longer there, the First National Bank of Yarmouth was located next to the two banks on the left side where the Cancer Shop is currently located.

In the background you see a collage of checks from T.T. Hallet's account dating back to the late 1880s.

Decorated for the town's tercentenary celebration in 1889, Allen Knowles house still remains as a prominent structure on Main St in Yarmouthport. Captain Allen Knowles commanded many vessels running from Liverpool to Boston. The Knowles lived there until 1971, and currently the Moeller family resides there.

One of the oldest houses in Yarmouthport, this house was built on 24 Old Kings Highway by Timothy Hallet, the grandson of Andrew Hallet, one of the original settlers of Yarmouth. Andrew came to Yarmouth in 1637 where he owned about 200 hundred acres of land.

Either Jonathan Hallet or his son, Thomas Hallet, built this home in the early 18th century believed to be on Wharf Lane. Upon Thomas' death, he gave the house to the son of his second wife, Joshua Gray.

Ansel Hallet's house resides off of Mill Lane where it overlooks Mill Pond. Captain Ansel Hallet was a pioneer in the packet industry, developing lines between Yarmouth and Boston. This house was built in 1798.

Shoveling Wharf Lane

In the late 1800s it was up to the citizens in Yarmouthport to clear and maintain the roadways to allow goods to be brought through. It also allowed the to access the main street of Yarmouthport where they could stock up on any supplies they may need over the long cold winter.

From the Chatham Celebration: Page 49: **Early Conditions**.

    The first occupation of the inhabitants was agriculture. They raised good crops of corn and rye, and also produced some wheat, flax and tobacco. Hay from the salt marshes was abundant. The cattle ran at large on the common lands; cattle marks were recorded in the town records. Sheep raising was an important industry, the wool being required for home use. Not long after 1860, the flocks had disappeared. Other subsistence was not hard to obtain. The waters were full of fish. The shores abounded in clams, quahogs and oysters. Scallops were not esteemed. Lobsters were abundant. Deer and other game roamed the woods, and seafowls were plentiful. Beach plums, wild grapes and cranberries and other berries abounded. Upon the settlement of the town the region was covered with pine forests, not without some oak, and in the swamps there was a considerable supply of cedar. The forests, no doubt, supplied the timber for the first houses, and considerable tar was made in the early years.

Located at the corner of Willow Street and 6A, formerly the Christmas Tree Shop, the house on the left is one of three buildings that were used. J.B. Hall, the building on the right, is believed to have moved to Dennis. The store sold furnishings, stoves, and hardware. Above is a receipt to the Yarmouth Weir Company for a pipe and a coffee pot for a mere $1.92.

"This Old Edson House" dates back to 1755. This old three-quarter Cape house stands at 43 Main Street in Yarmouthport where early records show that Eliphalet Edson lived there in 1810. He was a cabinetmaker who was married to Polly Johnson, a descendant of John and Priscilla Alden of the Mayflower Pilgrims. It is now the Abbicci Restaurant that was recently renovated in 2006. Little of the original building remains. This photo was taken during the late 1800s or early 1900s.

This shop of Fred Hallet & Co has been gone for quite some time now from Yarmouthport where it originally stood at the depot. The sign on the side promoted "Book and Job Printing," and he was certainly in the right spot in town for that. It was directly across Railroad Avenue (sometimes called Cross Street) from the depot, a short block away from Willow Street. It burned down several years ago, but his works still live on. Hallet's books and newspapers he published are still highly guarded by collectors and libraries. On the next page is an ad for Fred Hallet & Co. found in the 1895 directory of Barnstable, Yarmouth, and Dennis.

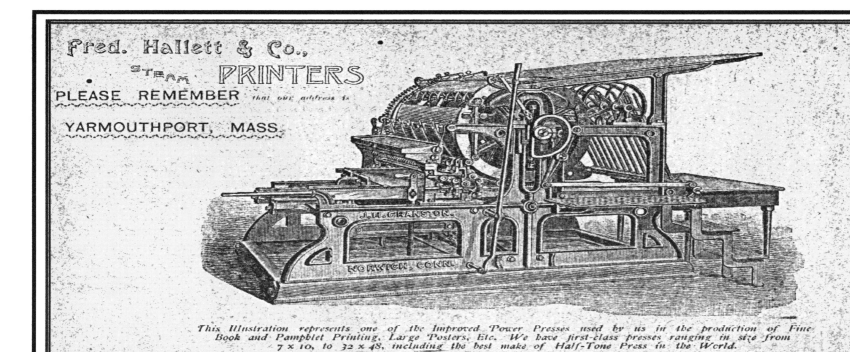

Now called *Anthony's Cummaquid*, the *Cummaquid Hotel* overlooks Mill Bridge and out towards Cape Cod bay. It's located on the Yarmouth-Barnstable town line on the North Shore. This photo displays that in the early 1900s not many trees covered the shoreline. Today trees cover the landscape. From here, you could see for miles. After it ceased to be a private home, it would then become an inn.

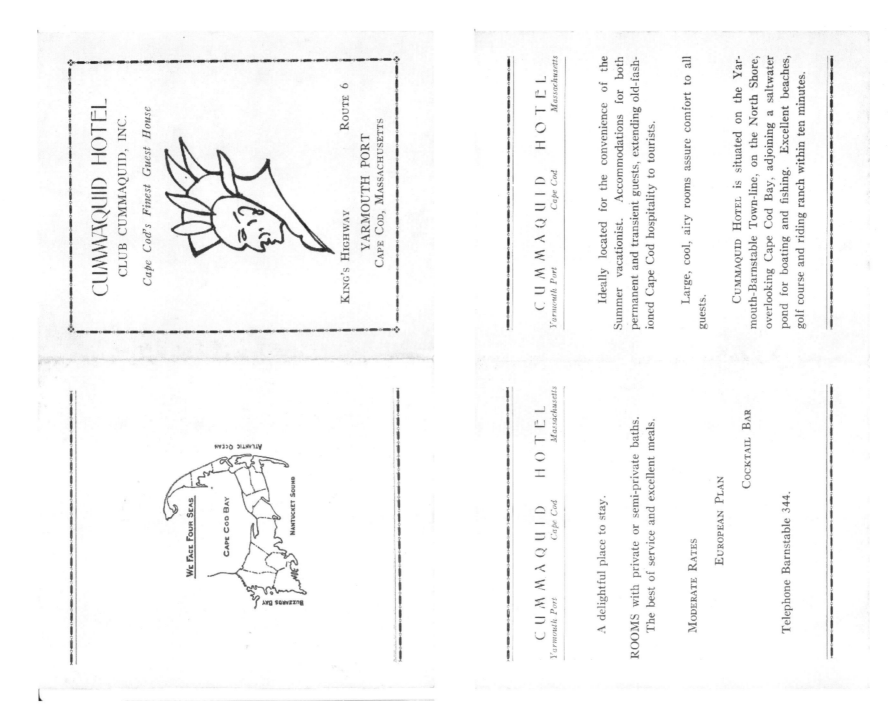

This is an exact copy of a Cummaquid Hotel brochure. Notice how the telephone number was only three numbers.

This is the view from Mill Lane looking towards the Cummaquid Inn. It sits on the Yarmouth-Barnstable line where it overlooks Cape Cod Bay. Beaches surround it, as do a golf course, and a riding ranch within 10 minutes of the hotel.

This is another view from Mill Lane looking towards the Cummaquid Inn. This massive structure sits a top one of the highest points of Hallet Pond, which merges with the ongoing ocean tides. The Cummaquid Inn has been known for years for its great dining view.

One of the earliest lumber companies on Cape Cod, Hinckley Lumber became a major supplier for a lot of the homes. They started in the Yarmouthport Depot, and would soon expand into Hyannis. Over the years, the company has endured through hard and poor times. Hinckley started out as a builder and then evolved into a supplier. As a family owned business, they also were involved in grain and hay. Trains would provide the area with a cheaper way to obtain goods, and the John Hinckley Co. took full advantage as wood products were brought in from various sites. As the building trade increased, and codes became more enforced, some of the building techniques they used in the mid 1800s are no longer used today. Have you heard of horsehair plaster? This was a way of adding horsehair to plaster to make it stronger. The Hinckley name exists today, as the Hinckley Home Center is located in Harwich.

This was John Hinckley's home in Cummaquid. The John Hinckley Lumber Company located in Hyannis, eventually merged with Nickerson Lumber to become one of the largest suppliers on the Cape.

This is another glass-plate photo of John Hinckley's home about 10 years later. Notice how the wooden fence has been replaced with a stone one. During the 1800s, all the rock had to be transported by horse and buggy since there were no trucks or other modern machinery.

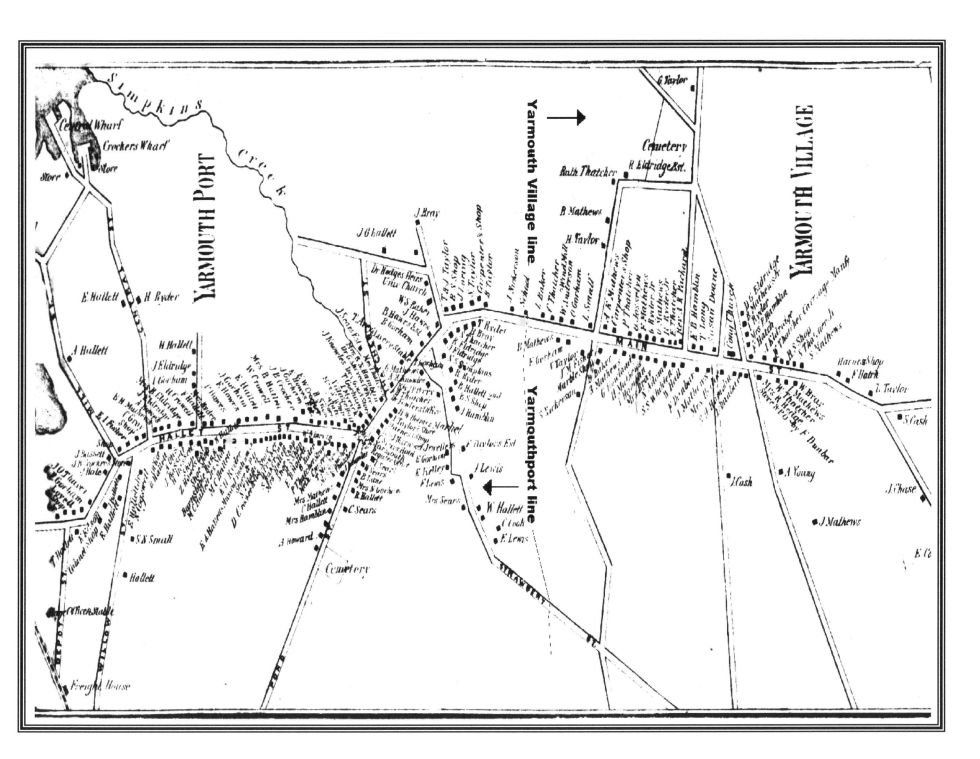

Barnstable

In Barnstable at 4380 Old Kings Highway, this is the New England Art Gallery. This home has gone through its fair share of changes; a barn is now there and the lawn view you see is now a parking lot.

This home is at an intersection at the entrance of Barnstable Village at 1780 Hyannis Road.
The sign reads: Hyannis 4 Mi, Centreville 5 Mi, Osterville 7 Mi.

Safari

Thacher Taylor Hallet on Safari

What kind of a person was Thacher Taylor Hallet? He virtually conquered Yarmouthport by being town selectman, tax collector, justice of the peace, collector of customs, pharmacist, and being an overall part of the high society. While digging deep into his legacy, it is astonishing to find out how much he was involved in. He was also a third degree Mason in the Fraternal Lodge of Massachusetts and was in charge of the poor by seeing they were fed and clothed. Hallet accomplished many things in his own town, but sought out greater things. Traveling would become a great passion of his and he went on adventures on safari overseas.

      During a time where large families were the norm, Hallet was very proud to have just one child to pass everything on to, naming his son after his father, that being Matthews C Hallet. On the next two pages you will see glass plates of what was given to Matthews by his father when he went on his safari adventures. Unlike today where you only need a cab ride to the airport to reach such destinations, it was of far greater time and challenge for Thacher Taylor. He would need to travel by horse and buggy to reach a train that took him to Yarmouthport to Boston, then to New York, which would then take him to a steamship or a boat. It is unclear of exactly when he traveled, but it is safe to say that all these ways of traveling were of primitive means. His intentions of these trips are also unknown, but due to his entrepreneurship, business was most likely the cause.

The native dress worn in the photo on the right was made from animal fur and pelts. Each tribe had their own unique headwear, and from the looks of the headdress and necklaces wore by the man in the photo on the left, he was of high rank. These are a set of glass plate photographs that T.T. Hallet had in his collection and are unusual for these types of photographs to surface on Cape Cod. It is unknown of what tribe these men belong too, but we do know that they were taken in the late 1800s.

The man on the left is holding a set of jewels. They may look like rocks, but they are diamonds set atop a leather glove. The picture on the right shows two mothers carrying their children in on their backs. Both photos show the working class of this particular tribe.

148

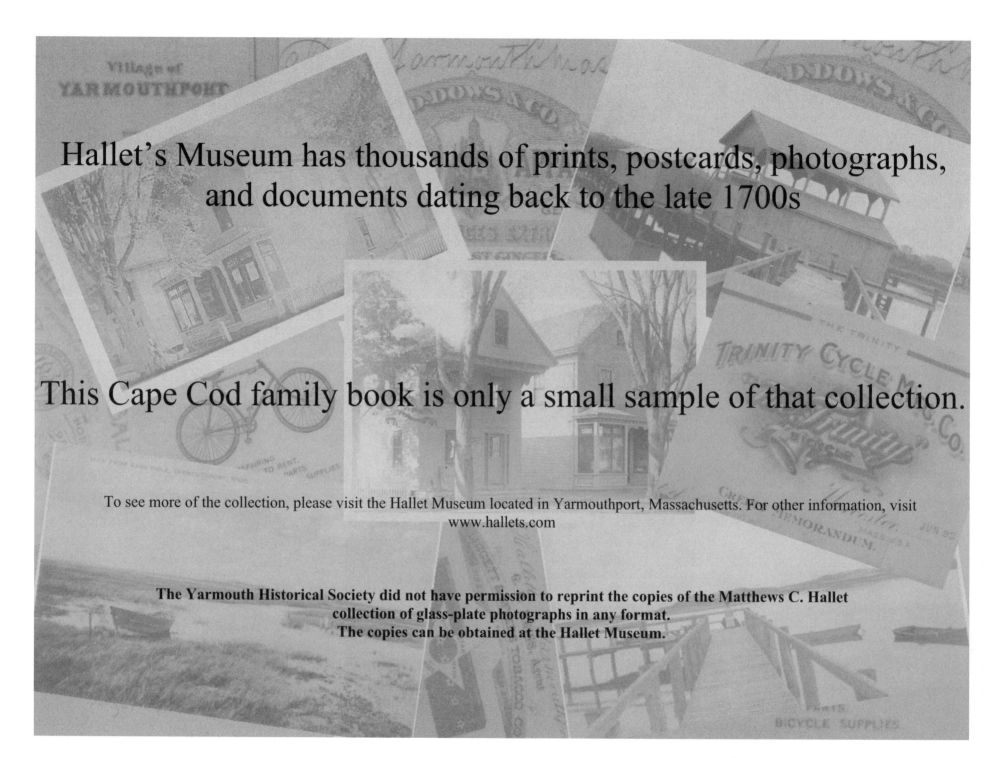

Hallet's Museum has thousands of prints, postcards, photographs, and documents dating back to the late 1700s

This Cape Cod family book is only a small sample of that collection.

To see more of the collection, please visit the Hallet Museum located in Yarmouthport, Massachusetts. For other information, visit www.hallets.com

H-1

H-4

H-7

H-2

H-5

H-8

H-3

H-6

H-9

151

H-10

H-13

H-16

H-11

H-14

H-17

H12

H-15

H-18

H-19

H-22

H-25

H-20

H-23

H-26

H-21

H-24

H-27

H-28

H-31

H-34

H-29

H-32

H-35

H-30

H-33

H-36

H-37

H-40

H-43

H-38

H-41

H-44

H-39

H-42

H-45

H-46

H-49

H-52

H-47

H-50

H-53

H-48

H-51

H-54

H-55

H-58

H-61

H-56

H-59

H-62

H-57

H-60

H-63

H-64

H-67

H-70

H-65

H-68

H-71

H-66

H-69

H-72

H-73

H-76

H-79

H-74

H-77

H-80

H-75

H-78

H-81

H-82

H-85

H-88

H-83

H-86

H-89

H-84

H-90

H-97

161

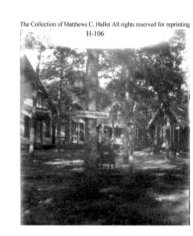

162

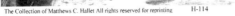

H-118

H-121

H-124

H-119

H-122

H-125

H-120

H-123

H-126

H-127

H-130

H-133

H-128

H-131

H-134

H-129

H-132

H-135

H-136

H-140

H-143

H-138

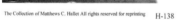

H-141

H-144

H-139

H-142

H-145

H-146

H-149

H-152

H-147

H-153

H-148

H-151

H-155

H-158

H-161

H-156

H-159

H-162

H-157

H-160

H-163

H-164

H-167

H-170

H-165

H-168

H-171

H-166

H-169

H-172

H-173

H-176

H-179

H-174

H-177

H-180

H-175

H-178

H-181

170

H-182

H-185

H-188

H-183

H-186

H-189

H-184

H-187

H-190

H-191

H-194

H-197

H-192

H-195

H-198

H-193

H-196

H-199

H-200

H-203

H-206

H-201

H-204

H-207

H-202

H-205

H-208

173

H-209

H-212

H-215

H210

H-213

H-216

H-211

174

H-217

H-227

H-229

H-231

H-228

H-230

H-232

176

177

Colonial Days

This flag is from about 1758 and is handmade by decedents of the Hallet family. It is uncertain if it is from the Howes, Taylors, or Crowells. It has been passed down though the years and was displayed opening day of the Hallet Museum in 1990, but has since been stored to preserve its fragile state. This flag was from the start of the thirteen colonies and symbolizes our land and newcomers to this nation. It was made prior to both the Civil War and Betsy Ross creating the American Flag as we know today.

The Interior of Hallet's store.

Taken around 1930, this picture shows the backdrop of the Hallet's Store soda fountain. The clock on the wall required constant maintenance and the soda fountain was in its heyday. The five-cent Cokes and the fifteen-cent ice cream cones were at an all-time high, and there were only seven flavors to choose from. Each town had it's own ice cream shop/pharmacy, as places similar to Hallet's were popular. Matt and Mary (photo on right) were making the most of this trend. She would make the sandwiches early in the morning, and he would tend to the newspapers and coffee. Like most businesses, this required long and enduring days, so they would take off and take an afternoon nap since their days would not end at 5 pm. As the summer season began, they would take upon their summer help. Their daughter Mary would work there as a child growing up. Years later, her sons Jon and Charles would work along side their grandparents.

In 1987, the contents of the store consisted of cigarettes, film, gum, razorblades, soap, shampoo, batteries, as well as personalized newspapers, with Mary writing the names of the customers on the newspapers for them. At the time, it was still allowed to smoke inside, so it was very common for customers to enjoy a cigarette with their morning coffee.

Mary Clark and Micki Quinn

by William P. Quinn

During my career as a cameraman for television news I frequently brought my granddaughter Micki with me for company. When the story was easy and quick she loved to ride around the Cape and enjoy the sights. I frequently stopped for lunch at Hallet's Store in Yarmouthport on Route 6A. It was a quick lunch, light, just a brownie and a coffee frappe shared with Micki. When she was young, I would give her a part of my brownie and some of the coffee frappe. Mary Clark was always behind the counter serving up my favorite lunch and came to know Micki quite well. She asked me once for a photo of Micki and I supplied her with some of the cute pictures I had made. Pretty soon there was quite a gallery of Micki's photos hanging on the shelf behind the counter. She was a cute little redhead and liked the attention given. Those photos stayed on the shelf until Mary passed away and she always liked them as she was the mother of four boys and never had a little girl herself.

In 1989, the town of Yarmouth celebrated its 350th birthday, and it was a great coincidence that Hallet's would be celebrating its 100th birthday on the same day.

The balloons were blown up, the banners were hung, the cake arrived, and the party began. Hallet's supplied 5-cent cokes and ice cream cones for the celebration. Television cameras arrived as the party was held out back where balloons were handed out and cokes were more or less given away despite the five-cent price. Dick Berch, a Hallet regular, was the one who arrived with the massive birthday cake to help with the celebration. Six-year old Sean Clark, the grandson of the owner, Mary Clark, was in charge of handing out the balloons.

With the banner outside reading "Happy Birthday," people wondered who's birthday it was. Some assumed it was Mary's, but the 61-year-old couldn't help but laugh when people told her she looked good for a 100-year-old.

Grace Snow and Barbara Davidson (on the right) volunteered for the day during this great celebration. They were former employees and good friends with Mary. Both knew everyone who came in the store, and many of the regulars arrived that day.

Hallet's t-shirts, sweatshirts, and hats were for sale. A secret untold by many, in the year of the celebration, there were only 100 hats made, so if you are one of the lucky ones to own one of them, you truly have a collector's item.

Photograph by William P. Quinn.

182

Yarmouth Port or Yarmouthport? Hallet or Hallett?

Which is the correct way of spelling Yarmouth Port/Yarmouthport? Are you a one 'T' Hallet or a two 'T' Hallett?

Bibliography

The Celebration of the Two Hundred and Fiftieth Anniversary of the Founding of Old Yarmouth, Mass.
Yarmouthport, Mass. Press of Fred Hallet. 1889.

The First Resident Directory of Barnstable, Yarmouth, and Dennis, Mass.
Quincy, Mass. The J.H. Hogan Company. 1895.

Yarmouth – An Historical Inventory.
Massachusetts. Yarmouth Historical Commission. 1980.

Beyle, Noel W.. The State of Cape Cod.
North Eastham, Mass. The First Encounter Press. 1979

Clark, Admont G. Lighthouses of Cape Cod-Martha's Vineyard-Nantucket: Their History and Lore
Parnassus Press. 1992.

Deyo, Simeon L., Editor, History of Barnstable County 1639-1890
New York. H.W, Blake and Co.   1890.

Swift, Charles F. History of Old Yarmouth
Yarmouthport, Mass. Charles F. Swift. 1884.

Quinn, William P. The Saltworks of Historic Cape Cod.
Orleans, Mass. Parnassus Imprints. 1993.

"Habits", "Railroads and other Public Means of Travel." The Chatham Celebration, 1712 to 1912. 1913: Page 56

All other information obtained from Mary G. Clark's research and the Hallet Museum.

Index of Pictures

65. Gorham Homestead – Main St., Yarmouth,P 57
66. Swift home on Main Street, Yarmouth across from Hallet Store,P 120
67. Pat Hannon and rig,P 80
68. unknown
69. House on Summer Street
70. Yarmouth Brass Band
71. Baker Girls house across from Yarmouthport Gallery
72. Flower field
73. Main Street – Yarmouth looking east in front of Hallet Store,P 86
74. unknown
75. David Thacher House on Thacher Shore Road-gone, P 106
76. Fred Grobe's home – moved across the street, P 117
77. Main Street, Yarmouth looking east (House #'s 496, 500, 502), P 82
78. Rick Jones house - Cummaquid
79. unknown
80. 5 generations – 1 family
81. Fred Grobe's home – moved across the street
82. Once Bill Sherman's house on 399 6A in Yarmouth, P 55
83. unknown
84. unknown
85. Once Richard Gilpin's house – 431 in Yarmouth 6A, P 54
86. Sadie Swift/Ed Bennett home – Hallet Street, Yarmouth

87. Edmund Walker, Wood Merchant, P 61
88. Sadie Swift/Ed Bennett home – Hallet Street, Yarmouth
89. House #201 and house before Lyceum Hall, Yarmouth,P 87
90. Harwood Palmer stuck in ice, Yarmouth 1905,P 24, 26
91. Main Street – Yarmouth, Hallet Cottage - beside the banks
92. Mill St., Bridge-water wagon, P 36
93. Ryder home in Cummaquid
94. Knowles house, Yarmouth, P 124
95. unknown
96. Main St., Yarmouth,P 88
97. Hallet's Drug Store P 119
98. Arthur Connelly's General Store, Yarmouthport,P 111
99. Main St., Yarmouth – Fred Hallet – gone now
100. Gorham house – Center Street, Yarmouth - House # 208
101. First National Bank of Yarmouth,P 123
102. Main St., Yarmouth, Crocker house and store, P 114
103. Adam's house
104. Unitarian Church afire - Barnstable, P 68
105. Driveway of Sandyside off Main St., Yarmouth,P 89
106. Yarmouth Campground, Hanover Square,P 73
107. Henry Abbott house, now Hayes
108. First National Bank of

Yarmouth,P 123
109. Davis house, Yarmouth
110. T.T. Hallet in front of Hallet's in 1928
111. Mill Bridge and Herbet Lovell's Fish Shanty,P 37
112.
113. Schoolhouse at fire station
114. Pier destroyed, P 23
115. Yarmouth Gristmill,P 72 - abandoned
116. Summer St., Dennis Pond
117. Loring Crocker saltworks,P 99
118. Bass River, windmill at golf course,P 94
119. Sears Manor, Summer St., P 109
120. unknown
121. unknown
122. David Thacher House - gone
123. Saltworks, Mill Bridge,P 97
124. unknown
125. 6A and Summer Street,P 108
126. Edmund Walker – Wood Merchant
127. Across the street from Yarmouth Art Gallery
128. Yarmouth Methodist Campground,P 73
129. On 6A, house #'s 424 and 425
130. Cape Cod Bay
131. Inlet
132. unknown
133. unknown
134. 361 on 6A – Gorham Family
135. Plate
136. Sears Manor on Summer Street, P109

137.
138. Hallet relative
139. unknown
140. Garden
141. Wildflowers
142. 143 6A – Gingerbread house, P 121
143. unknown
144. family unknown
145. Artifact
146. Jacobs Sears Library in Dennis, P 47
147. 6A – Christmas Tree Shop & J.B. Hall
148. House #24 on 6A,P 125
149. Barn with flowers
150. unknown
151. Today is the Abbicci Restaurant
152. Yarmouth near Railroad Ave
153. Llamas
154. Woman in parlor - unknown
155. Man with flowers in barn
156. R. Spencer painting, P 30
157. R. Spencer painting,P 31
158. May Russell Howes/Thacher
159. Woman sitting in front of fireplace,P 13
160. unknown members of Hallet family
161. Interior of Aiken home,P 76
162/163. Moved to First Congressional Church,P 69
164. unknown
165. unknown
166. Chandler Gray House, corner-Wharf Lane
167. 450 6A next to park,P 51

168. unknown
169. 438 6A, now Blueberry Manor,P 52
170. Sears Manor on Summer St., P 109
171. 1780 Hyannis Rd - Barnstable, P 144
172. Old Yarmouth Inn

173. Cummaquid Inn looking from Mill Pond, P 137
174. Ships on Cape Cod Bay,P 27
175. Llamas
176. unknown members of Hallet
177. unknown
178. unknown
179. May Russell Howes/Thacher
180. unknown family
181. unknown
182. Sturges house
183. unknown
184. unknown
184. unknown
185. unknown
186. unknown
187. 194 6A, now a child's boutique
188. May Russell Howes/Thacher
189. unknown
190. 189 Center St,P 53
191. Fred Grobe's home on 146 6A, P 118
192 – 198. Fireplace with painting, P 59
199. unknown
200. House in Cummaquid
201. unknown
202. unknown

203. Picture of a Valley
204. Gorham house at the end of Center Street - - House # 208
205. Gorham house at the end of Center Street - House # 208
206. unknown
207. unknown
208. unknown
209. unknown
210. unknown
211. unknown
212. Gorham house at the end of Center Street - House # 208
213. Summer Street
214. Ansel Hallet home on Mill Ln.
215. Henry Abbott house, now Hayes
216. Dave Swift's home
217. unknown
218. Dave Swift's home
219. Corner of 6A and Mill Lane
220. Daniel Crocker home – # 159 on 6A
221. 6A – after P 201
222. Gorham house at the end of Center St.
223. Chandler Gray House, corner of Wharf Lane
224. Building and Post office at Yarmouth Methodist Camp Grounds,P 74
225. unknown
226. unknown
227. Goodell House – George Adams, Wharf Lane
228. unknown

Index

#'s

W

Walker, Edmund, 60, 61
Walking Plank, 17
Weir Road, 49
weir, 17, 18, 19
Whale's Tooth, The, 11
Wharf Lane, 2, 18, 24, 32, 38, 126, 128
wharf, 2, 17, 18, 20, 24, 32, 38, 41, 101, 126, 128
White, Otis, 18
Willow Street, 62, 63, 73, 130, 132
windmill, 71, 94
World War II, 1, 33

Y

Yacht, 101
Yarmouth Methodist Campground, 73, 74
Yarmouth Register, 3, 81
Yarmouth Register, The 110, 120
Yarmouth Weir Company, 130
Yarmouth, 1, 2, 3, 8, 9, 15, 17, 18, 25, 33, 36, 39, 41, 46, 48, 50, 51, 53, 54, 57, 66, 67, 68, 69, 71, 72, 74, 82, 83, 95, 96, 108, 115, 122, 125, 127, 132, 134, 136, 141, 150, 182, 183
Yarmouthport, 1, 2, 3, 6, 8, 10, 12, 17, 26, 52, 56, 67, 75, 81, 84, 85, 87, 97, 98, 104, 105, 110, 114, 115, 116, 117, 118, 119, 124, 125, 128, 131, 132, 138, 141, 146, 150, 181, 183